YALE SCHOOL OF ARCHITECTURE

YALE SCHOOL OF ARCHITECTURE
EDWARD P. BASS DISTINGUISHED VISITING ARCHITECTURE FELLOWSHIP

URBAN INTERSECTIONS: SÃO PAULO

KATHERINE FARLEY / DEBORAH BERKE

Edited by Nina Rappaport, Noah Biklen, and Eliza Higgins

Published by
Yale School of Architecture
180 York Street
New Haven, Connecticut 06520
www.architecture.yale.edu

Distributed by
W. W. Norton & Company Inc.
500 Fifth Avenue
New York, New York 10110
www.wwnorton.com

This book was made possible through the Edward P. Bass Distinguished Visiting Architecture Fellowship fund of the Yale School of Architecture.
It is the sixth in a series of publications of the Bass fellowship published through the dean's office.

Edited by Nina Rappaport, Yale School of Architecture Publications Director, Noah Biklen and Eliza Higgins

Copy Editors: David Delp and Jamie Chan

Portugese translation: Gabriel Köche Cé and Karini Machado

Design: mgmt. design, Brooklyn, New York

Cover: São Paulo photograph by Noah Biklen

Library of Congress Cataloging-in-Publication Data

Farley, Katherine.

Urban intersections : São Paulo / Katherine Farley, Deborah Berke ; edited by Nina Rappaport, Noah Biklen and Eliza Higgins.

p. cm. – (Edward P. Bass Distinguished Visiting Architecture Fellowship ; 6)

ISBN 978-0-393-73352-5 (pbk.)

1. City planning–Brazil–São Paulo. 2. Mixed-use developments–Brazil–São Paulo–Planning. 3. Architecture–Study and teaching–Connecticut–New Haven. 4. São Paulo (Brazil)–Buildings, structures, etc.–Designs and plans. I. Berke, Deborah. II. Rappaport, Nina. III. Biklen, Noah K. IV. Higgins, Eliza. V. Title.

NA9166.S3F37 2011

711'.4098161--dc23

2011034426

CONTENTS

Edward P. Bass Distinguished Visiting Architecture Fellowship In 2003, Edward P. Bass, a 1967 graduate of Yale College who studied at the Yale School of Architecture as a member of the class of 1972, endowed this fellowship to bring property developers to the school to lead advanced studios in collaboration with design faculty. Mr. Bass is an environmentalist who sponsored the Biosphere 2 development in Oracle, Arizona, in 1991, and a developer responsible for the ongoing revitalization of the downtown portion of Fort Worth, Texas, where his Sundance Square, which combines restoration with new construction, has transformed a moribund urban core into a vibrant regional center. In all his work, Mr. Bass has been guided by the conviction that architecture is a socially engaged art operating at the intersection of grand visions and everyday realities.

The Bass fellowship ensures that the school curriculum recognizes the role of the property developer as an integral part of the design process. The fellowship brings developers to Yale to work side by side with educators and architecture students in the studio, situating the discussion about architecture in the wider discourse of contemporary practice. The first Bass studio, led by Gerald Hines and Louis I. Kahn Visiting Professor Stefan Behnisch, in 2005, was documented in *Poetry, Property, and Place* (2006). The second Bass studio, in 2006, which teamed Stuart Lipton with Saarinen Visiting Professor Sir Richard Rogers ('62), engineer Chris Wise, and architect Malcolm Smith ('97), was documented in *Future-Proofing* (2007). *The Human City* (2008) records the Yale Studio collaboration of Roger Madelin and Bishop Visiting Professor Demetri Porphyrios. *Urban Integration: Bishopsgate Goods Yard,* which documents the studio led by Nick Johnson and the FAT architecture partnership, was published in 2009, and, in 2010, Charles Atwood and architect David M. Schwarz's studio work was published in *Learning in Las Vegas.* With this sixth book in the series it is a pleasure to present the research and studio led by real estate developer Katherine Farley and longtime Yale School of Architecture adjunct professor Deborah Berke, both of New York City.

Preface: Robert A.M. Stern, Dean *Urban Intersection: São Paulo* documents the sixth architect-developer studio to be conducted at Yale, led in spring 2010 by Edward P. Bass Distinguished Visiting Fellow Katherine Farley, Senior Managing Director of Tishman Speyer—one of the world's most respected developers—and Deborah Berke, adjunct professor at Yale, who challenged students to design a new large-scale, high-density apartment development complex on a key site in the heart of São Paulo, Brazil. Farley, a graduate of Brown University and of the Harvard Graduate School of Design, is responsible for the firm's work in Brazil and China as well as its global marketing. After a degree in architecture she worked for Ameristone, a division of Turner International and joined Tishman Speyer in 1984, where she has been a managing director since 1998. Farley has also contributed to New York City's cultural life as a board member of Lincoln Center for the Performing Arts since 2003, and as chair of the Lincoln Center Development Project. She was also chair of the Real Estate Committee of the New York Philharmonic Orchestra and on the board of the Lincoln Center Theater. She serves on the Board of Overseers of the International Rescue Committee and is chairman emeritus of Women in Need.

Deborah Berke founded her New York City based firm Deborah Berke & Partners Architects in 1982. She received her architecture degree from Rhode Island School of Design (RISD) and a masters degree in urban design from City College. In 2005, she was awarded an honorary doctorate from RISD. She has been teaching architecture at Yale since 1987 and had previously taught at the University of Maryland, Rhode Island School of Design, the University of Miami, and The Institute for Architecture and Urban Studies where she was a fellow. Her projects include numerous residences, the renovation and addition to the Yale School of Art, the conversion of PS 122 into an arts center in New York. For Marlboro College, Berke developed a master plan and designed the Serkin Center. She has also prepared the campus plan for the European College of Liberal Arts in Berlin. Yale University Press published a monograph of her work in 2009.

I wish to thank Katherine Farley and Deborah Berke for their dedication to the studio. As well, I wish to express my appreciation to Noah Biklen ('03), who assisted with its organization and to Nina Rappaport, Publications Director at the Yale School of Architecture, who with Biklen and Eliza Higgins ('10), one of the students in the studio, co-edited *Urban Intersections: São Paulo.*

Introduction: Nina Rappaport, Noah Biklen, and Eliza Higgins, editors São Paulo is a fast-changing city replete with new high-rise developments that contrast sharply with the organic growth of favelas on the hillsides, a disparity made more obvious by limited connections between the economically divided districts. While economical and environmental design has long been a part of Brazilian architecture, it is only recently that sustainable practices have been applied to the scale and performance objectives of new developments.

A Yale studio led by Edward P. Bass Distinguished Visiting Architecture Fellow Katherine Farley, a Senior Managing Director at Tishman Speyer, with Yale professor and architect Deborah Berke, proposed that the students design a middle-income residential development. Initially, students found it difficult to comprehend the site, but it and the cultural conditions of São Paulo became clearer after a weeklong visit to the city led by Farley at which time they presented their preliminary designs to the São Paulo-based Tishman development team. Back in New Haven projects were then developed in detail and were presented at term end to a panel of architects, developers, and journalists.

This book opens with a conversation between Katharine Farley and Deborah Berke about development and design and their careers, followed by an essay, "RMSP," by architectural critic Vanessa Grossman, who sorts out ways to understand the city's developmental history and addresses the challenges facing contemporary architects. This is followed by the documentation of the student work beginning with their site analyses, continuing with the individual student projects. Some students proposed compositions of residential towers that considered security, ecology, amenities, and the relationship to the surrounding neighborhoods. Others used landscape as an organizing strategy, taking into account seasonal transformations, water flow, prevailing winds, and circulation as a framework. Students incorporated performative architectonic elements, such as modular shading panels and voided interior spaces to create distinctive qualities. Most of all, students worked to give the neighborhood project form, analyzing buildings in relationship to new neighborhoods and community services, or gardens with topographic landscapes that contrasted with characteristic superblocks of Brazilian Modernism.

The book closes with excerpts from the final jury review with Patrick Bellew, Andy Bow, Peggy Deamer, Tom Farrell, Sean Griffiths, Audrey Matlock ('79), Cathleen McGuigan, Rob Rogers, Annabelle Selldorf, and Claire Weisz ('89) as they discussed ethical development, sustainability, and affordability in the changing Brazilian economy, and final comments by Deborah Berke.

The editors would like to acknowledge the work of the students who participated in the studio and whose cooperation was essential to this book: Bradley Baer ('11), Lis Cena ('11), Rebecca Garnett ('10), Carmel Greer ('10), Alejandro Fernandez de Mesa ('10), Eliza Higgins ('10), Catherine Anderson Poulin ('10), Anja Turowski ('10), Steve Ybarra ('10), and Hilary Zaic ('10).

We also extend our appreciation to the work of Gabriel Köche Cé and Karini Machado, who translated the book into Portuguese. Copy editors David Delp and Jamie Chan deserve acknowledgement as do graphic designers Sarah Gephart and Tracey Chan of mgmt. design, New York for their elegant work.

I. THE VA
DESIGN:
DIALOGU

I. O VALOR DO DESIGN: O DIÁLOGO

LUE OF
IN
E

Opposite: Foster + Partners architects, Tishman Speyer developers, Hearst Headquarters, New York City, 2006.
Oposta: Foster + Partners, arquitetos, Tishman Speyer empreendedores, Sede da Hearst, Nova Iorque, 2006.

Katherine Farley and **Deborah Berke** discuss their work and teaching with architectural critic Nina Rappaport.

Nina Rappaport Katherine, what inspired you to teach in an architecture school? You are trained as an architect, but had you ever taught in the field before?

Katherine Farley I felt that it is important for architects to train not only in design but to build our designs. If an architectural education doesn't include training in the skills necessary to take a design idea through the development-and-construction obstacle course, then architects will not be prepared to get their designs built. The mission of the studio was to expose the students to the consideration of a real-life project execution.

NR How did you become a female pioneer in the field of real estate development? What was it like when you first started working with a construction company?

KF I remember, in my first interview, they said, "We have 3,200 employees—would you like to meet the other one?" It was a wake-up call but also a great experience. I think my most significant role models were the people I met in China. Their negotiating styles were more comfortable to me than those I saw in a typical U.S. construction negotiation. I learned a lot by observing how they worked. These days, there are many more women in the American design, development, and construction business—although never enough—and, more and more, we see women assuming senior roles in international business as well.

NR Deborah, your work has often focused on both institutional and art-related projects. What are your current projects, and how have you conceptualized them?

Deborah Berke We are working on many interesting projects right now that range from houses to institutional buildings for the arts. These include a performing-arts project at SUNY Fredonia, a music conservatory at Bard College, and a film-studies building at North Carolina School of the Arts. We are also doing two hotels, in Arkansas and in Ohio, that are further developments of the 21c Museum Hotel brand we started in Louisville, Kentucky, several years ago. Then, in New York City, we are working on a publicly funded arts project, the extensive renovation of 122CC, a former public school long used to house arts organizations from Mabou Mines and Performance Space 122 to Painting Space 122 and exhibition space. This is a Department of Design and Construction Design Excellence project. Construction is expected to begin this year. We are continuing our work for the European College of Liberal Arts, in Berlin; the campus is made up of several former embassies in the Pankow neighborhood, in the former East Berlin. Our master plan proposed a way to connect the disparate buildings to form a campus, as well as build additions and new structures to meet the college's needs. We are now moving ahead on the first of these buildings.

Opposite: Botti-Rubin Arquitectos Associados architects, Tishman Speyer developers, North Tower (tallest tower).
Oposta: Botti-Rubin Arquitectos Associados arquitetos, Tishman Speyer empreendedores, Torre Norte (torre mais alta).

NR It has been interesting to see how some of the developers teaching in the Yale Bass fellowship studios over the past four years—such as Roger Madelin, of Argent, in London—have used a certain philosophy to guide their employees. For example, Madelin's firm's concept is "Principles for a New Human City." Does Tishman Speyer have a philosophy that it uses to build projects around the world, in places such as India, Brazil, and China? What is your vision for urban design in diverse cultures?

KF Yes, we do have a philosophy: excellence. We develop buildings that represent excellence, a definition that changes both over time and because of the market. We believe a high-quality building is the last to suffer in a downturn and the first to recover. Buildings of this caliber attract the best tenants and have the most risk-protected revenue stream. We hire top executives who are committed to excellence in our buildings, our people, and our standards of professionalism. Our buildings don't look the same in every market. Each building is designed to suit the particular tenant requirements of the specific market. We develop what is considered the very top of whatever market we are in. For instance, in Brazil fifteen years ago, the local market defined a Class A space in a certain way. When we constructed our first building in Brazil, the local market began to refer to it as a Class AA space.

NR What projects are you most proud of?

KF I would say the MesseTurm, in Frankfurt, designed by Helmut Jahn, which was our first international project and the tallest building in Europe at the time. The North Tower, our first project in Brazil designed by a local architecture firm, Botti Rubin Arquitetos, set the new standard for office quality that I mentioned earlier. Since then, we have finished the first two green projects in South America; one was designed by a local architect, Aflalo e Gasperini Arquitetos, and the second was a beautiful project in Rio designed by KPF.

NR How do you incorporate sustainability into these large-scale projects? Is that part of your standard moving forward?

KF As a company, we understand that the world of sustainability is evolving, and we like to think that we are in the forefront of addressing those issues. Many things, from the technology to the willingness of tenants to pay for it, are evolving. Probably the most significant building we have completed is the Hearst Tower, by Sir Norman Foster, which was the first Gold LEED building in Manhattan. Although it was not one that I had a lot of personal involvement in, I'm very proud of it.

NR How have you used your architectural background in your projects? For example, how do you guide the design of a project?

BCN
BCN
D&D

Opposite: KPF, Aflalo e Gasperini Arquitetos, Tishman Speyer developers, Ventura Corporate Headquarters (building with notch).
Oposta: KPF, Aflalo e Gasperini arquitetos, Tishman Speyer empreendedores, sede da Ventura Corporate (edifício com entalhe).

KF Development is all about choices. Given that no project's budget is infinite, we are engaged in a process of prioritizing design elements and choosing those that will be most meaningful to the building design and to the users in the market. My training as an architect has been invaluable in this process.

NR Deborah, the timing of this studio relates to your recent work with larger developers that are more focused on the bottom line. How do you continue to maintain design standards under that constraint?

DB I am working with developers on projects in New York City, and for the 21c Museum Hotels, with one completed in Louisville, Kentucky, and three more under way. I like when the challenges presented by a tight budget play out in a dialogue that helps to shape the work. That relationship informs the design process in a way that is different from the dialogue in institutional work. I maintain standards by being able to successfully argue the role of design in defining "brand" and creating value.

NR What do you think makes a good developer? Are you interested in the business side of development projects?

DB Not really, but I don't mean that in a cavalier way. I understand that the numbers have to work and that is a positive constraint, especially with a "good" developer. A good developer doesn't necessarily throw more money at a project but understands the necessity of making budget choices informed by design.

NR Have you ever surprised a developer by incorporating more elegant design features while reducing costs?

DB Our building at 48 Bond Street in New York City is a great example. It sold out before the competition on the block did, and it tested the model. The developer wanted to work with an architect but was still driven by the bottom line. We sold him on the big idea, which was the nature of the façade. At a certain point—and I think this is true with all of my work—I would rather spend a little money in some areas of a project and lots of money in others, rather than spending modest amounts everywhere. That was a strategy we tested on Bond Street with the façade, the swimming pool, and certain aspects of the apartments—we indulged in costly design ideas in some areas by spending less in others.

NR Katherine, what do you consider a good working relationship between you and architects, and how do you direct the design? What part of the process do you enjoy the most?

KF I think the design process is most successful when you have a knowledgeable and talented architect with a strong point of view who also understands that a successful project has many other aspects beyond pure design

Opposite: Deborah Berke Architects, 48 Bond Street, New York City, 2008.
Oposto: Deborah Berke Arquitetos, Rua Bond número 48, Nova Iorque, 2008.

that have to be accommodated. On the one hand, you don't want an architect who says, "Just tell me what to do and I'll do it." But on the other hand, you don't want an architect who is dogmatic and thinks there is only one way to solve a problem. It's very exciting to be part of an integrated team representing various different kinds of expertise, coming together to address development challenges, with the shared objective of developing a great project.

NR How do you select architects and put together a team locally for projects such as the North Tower, in Brazil, designed by Botti Rubin Arquitetos? What advantages has having a local team brought to your development projects?

KF When we open offices abroad, we build a Tishman Speyer team that is primarily local. They speak the local language and are from the local culture but are also part of the Tishman Speyer global and professional culture. Across the company there are consistent best practices on both design and technical issues. We work hard at being a global company rather than just a regional franchise. In Brazil, for example, we initially used a combination of local and international architects and accepted a certain amount of redundancy in the beginning to be sure that we could deliver the international quality our tenants would expect from us. As we have gained experience in Brazil, we have increasingly used local architects, although we often still have the participation of international architects.

NR What is your role in these overseas projects? Do you influence the selection of the architect and the site?

KF Over the years my role has varied, but it has included at various times both the startup and the overall regional responsibility for Germany, France, Argentina, and India. Today I am responsible for our business in Brazil and China. In this role I am deeply involved in all aspects of the business, including site acquisition and selection of architects, among other things. Before we select an architect, we discuss ideas with both the local team and the design and construction department at our New York City headquarters. As the project develops, the local team works daily with the architect, and I check in frequently for design and overall project reviews. In our design reviews, we have our leasing, marketing, design, construction, and property management experts comment on the design from all aspects of development, including construction, feasibility, and cost.

NR Deborah, why have the 21c hotels been so successful both financially and in terms of design strategy?

DB It is an amazing hotel experience. The rooms and public spaces are designed carefully. We are not hotel architects, so we brought in a different set of eyes for the interiors. The owners are not hotel developers; we didn't have a formulaic hotel design, and they didn't want one. Their first goal was for the hotel to contribute to the renaissance of downtown Louisville, Kentucky. The success was a surprise and a delight. The integration of the art into the hotel is

Opposite: Deborah Berke Architects, 21c Museum Hotel, Louisville, Kentucky, 2006.
Oposta: Deborah Berke Arquitetos, 21c Hotel Museu, Louisville, Kentucky, 2006.

absolutely genuine; it is not a marketing strategy or a branding idea. The owners are serious collectors who want to share their collection. Their specific vision infuses the hotel experience, and the art is real. I think people intuitively understand that.

NR How are you coping with the changes in the economic environment? And with that in mind, how would you advise architectural students?

KF In challenging economic times it is more important than ever for students to understand the other perspectives that come into play in developing buildings. A successful architect needs to be skillful in areas way beyond pure design and understand the relationship between design and financial, technical, timing, and even political and macroeconomic issues. The objective of the studio was also to help architects understand how to prioritize those issues so that the most meaningful aspects of the design intent are preserved even under times of economic pressure.

NR What was most challenging about the studio site?

DB The project is on a complex site with a significant slope and a not-very-good historic building that needs to be saved, and the site borders a variety of different neighborhoods. Some of the design issues include defining what kind of place it will be as it is approached from different areas, as well as coming up with solutions for difficulty of access. The overall picture—and what is most interesting—is that it is a middle-class residential project. While the problem of housing the poor in emerging countries is of enormous significance, it is not something you can address in a developer studio. It is a governmental issue. But we are asking the students to look at the housing component and then add mixed uses. What can you add to the program that is appropriate to its position in the city and to your aspirations for it? And if you make housing, what goes with it—sports facilities, a school, a library? We cannot think in terms of American-style amenities to sell the housing. Instead, we ask, what will make it a better place to live? The idea of the studio was not to design complete residential units but rather for the students to think about the nature of the community they are creating.

KF They were evaluated on how they solved the design problem as well as how responsive their solution was to a variety of development challenges, including sustainability, marketability, and construction feasibility. We also did a simplified version of a costing exercise, and students learned to address real-world development trade-offs. For example, they saw that the choice of an expensive glass curtain wall makes it challenging to achieve the desired sustainability rating, and a certain amount more in rent would be needed for the project to be viable commercially. Discussions with market experts helped them determine whether the additional value of that design decision

Opposite: Deborah Berke Architects, Marianne Boesky Gallery, New York City, 2009.
Oposta: Deborah Berke Arquitetos, Galeria Marianne Boesky, Nova Iorque, 2009.

would be appreciated enough in the market by the tenants to warrant that choice. As they weighed the options, we discussed the intangible value of so-called trophy buildings, where tenants do pay more in rent for a building with an excellent design.

NR Most of the other developer studios have focused on master-planning frameworks for large development sites, with the students designing buildings in a more schematic and less detailed architectural scheme. How much did you want completely designed buildings to enter into the concepts?

DB This studio went through the master-plan phase rather quickly and then got to a smaller piece of it so the students could make buildings. I was interested in the parts at the intersection of communal and residential programs. Students didn't have to design each unit, but it was interesting to see the impact of the master plan on each facility and what the relationship is between the community and the building.

NR What did you hope the students learned that they wouldn't normally be exposed to in an architect-led studio?

DB I think the back and forth between disciplines illustrated the trade-offs between cost and design. It is important that students understand the pressures entailed in development. It will make them better architects as well as contribute more profoundly to the built environment as a whole.

II. THE DE
ING CITY
SÃO PAU

II. A CIDADE EM DESENVOLVIMENTO: SÃO PAULO

EVELOP-

LO

RMSP: METRO-POLITAN REGION OF SÃO PAULO

RMSP: REGIÃO METROPOLITANA DE SÃO PAULO

Vanessa Grossman, architectural critic and historian, discusses the challenges of infrastructure and development in São Paulo providing a context for the studio.

"A friend recently told me he had traversed the region of the Harz, in Germany, using a street map of London whose instructions he had blindly followed. This kind of game is nothing but a poor start of what could be a complete construction of architecture and urbanism."[1] Here, following the ideas of Guy Debord's friend, I will drift into Paris and use one of its maps in order to conduct my reader to a location on the other side of the Atlantic, the so-called Região Metropolitana de São Paulo (São Paulo Metropolitan Region, or RMSP).

While drifting through Paris in the late 1950s, the Situationist Debord came to believe that cities have a psychogeographical image, with constant currents, fixed points, and vortexes that strongly encourage attraction to or repulsion from certain zones. He developed what he named "*cartes psychogégographiques*," or "psychogeographic maps," for which the conception of a map as an implicit act of possession of territory was replaced by the representation of erratic paths, atmospheres, and subjective disorders. Disintegrating the sovereign unity of the city, his 1956 *Guide Psychogéographique de Paris* consisted of a collection of selected urban fragments of Paris representing a subjectively recomposed urban space. However, Debord was dissatisfied with not only the cartographical skills of mapmakers but also the work of architects and urban planners. The fragments represented were mainly those about to disappear vis-à-vis the urbanization of Paris since World War II. One of the consequences of this process was the formation of the suburbs.

Almost sixty years afterward, this process of urbanization reached a stage of consolidation. Despite the presence of the *Périphérique*—the highway encircling central Paris between the city and its suburbs—what is labelled as "greater Paris" remains a sovereign unity in terms of its infrastructure and even in the "mental map" of its inhabitants. There are differences in the quality of its urban spaces as well as in the scale of its distances. Yet the Paris subway map, for example, provides its users with a good sense of greater Paris's whole: its extensions, limits, and accessibility.

If I have stopped short of a consideration of the psychogeographical representation of a city by its fragments, it is because it seems to me that what could be described as a Situationist urban subjectivity objectively came through in other locations of the globe, where different socio-political circumstances took place. One of these regions would be the RMSP, where fragmentation is not an abstraction but an urban condition. The Brazilian architects and urban planners Leandro Medrano and Luiz Recamán read the formation of this urban agglomeration, where planning has often existed but has been rarely implemented, as "an endless process of juxtaposition, discontinuity, and fragmentation, transforming the whole city into a self-engulfing movement of value production and segregation."[2]

The Tietê River frequently bursts its banks, flooding major highways constructed along them.

O Rio Tietê frequentemente rompe suas margens, inundando grandes rodovias construídas ao longo.

The Anhangabaú Valley, one of São Paulo's canalized rivers, in one of the oldest parts of the city. In this case, the river was transformed into a public square under which a tunnel connects the north and south zones of the RMSP.
O Vale do Anhangabaú, um dos Rios canalizados de São Paulo, em uma das partes mais antigas da cidade. Neste caso, o rio foi transformado em uma praça pública e debaixo dela um túnel conecta as zonas norte e sul da RMSP.

In fact, this process is a recent development, as the RMSP did not exist before 1973.[3] It consists of 39 municipalities, 38 of which are grouped around the state capital, São Paulo, and are directly or indirectly polarized by it.

It represents 3.4 percent of the total territory of the state of São Paulo, with an area of 8,051 square kilometers, or 3,108.508 square miles, in which 48.04 percent of the state's population is concentrated.[4] It is characterized by a significant conurbation of areas belonging to different municipalities, a concentration of population of about 19.7 million, and development of a complex system of concentrated centers of tertiary activities at various levels.

The RMSP started to expand rapidly, especially after the 1970s, when a huge contingent of population from the northeast of Brazil started to migrate to São Paulo with no ability to afford the increasing price of the urban land. This new migratory wave gave birth to a non-orchestrated process of urban growth, marked by shortages in all senses: in terms of social housing, mostly characterized by auto-construction; in terms of urbanization and infrastructure, with the formation of *favelas* (shanty towns) and *periferias* (the suburbs), both distinguished by clandestine land subdivision development; and in terms of public transportation, complemented by the circulation of clandestine vans, called *peruas,* that operate in areas where the official transportation system does not reach. If the inhabitants of *favelas* represented one percent of São Paulo's population in the beginning of the 1970s, they represented twenty percent in the beginning of the 1990s.[5]

In this sense, one could argue that architects and urban planners did not design a significant part of the RMSP, and, consequently, territorial discontinuity, auto-construction, and a spatially manifested class segregation are three of its hallmarks. Using Kevin Lynch's concepts for inhabitants to produce a map of the RMSP independently of his or her social class,[6] this map would be psychogeographic. It would be a guide to only selected zones of the RMSP because none of its inhabitants have access to all the numerous fragments composing the megacity's discontinuous urban fabric.

And yet São Paulo has been the object of successive urban planning and legislation that have not always been followed or implemented. The most recent, the *Plano Diretor Estratégico do Município de São Paulo,* or "the strategic master plan of São Paulo," approved in September 2002 and valid until 2012, has been polemically discussed and debated ever since its approval. An exception was one of São Paulo's first structural urban plans, which ended up informing the metropolitan expansion. This plan refers back to the 1930s, when Prestes Maia, one of the city's most renowned urban planners and mayors, decided to espouse the automobile in his so-called *Plano de Avenidas*, or "Plan of the Avenues." What was conceived as a structural solution generated some of the RMSP's main structural problems as a consequence of the marriage between a system entirely based on the automobile and the lack of investment in public transportation, both characteristics of most Brazilian cities.

In addition, the various valleys, which once served to drain the city's sewage, were transformed into large roadways for increased traffic. Gradually, the old meadows provided space for highways, not parks or public facilities. This process of sealing the area's natural ability to absorb rainwater has been aggravated by the fact that, in the last decades, unplanned sectors often occupy the areas of springs, rivers, and streams of a catchment basin, the drainage systems of which have also been affected by climate change.[7] As a consequence, floods still constitute one of the major problems of the city in RMSP today.

In terms of urban planning, since 1912, the City of São Paulo Improvements and Freehold Land Company Ltd best known in Brazil as "Cia City," has been another strong presence in São Paulo. This company, founded by the French architect Joseph Bouvard with French, British, and Brazilian investors, was attentive to the directions in which São Paulo expanded, especially in terms of its main activities and infrastructure during the first decades of the twentieth century. Therefore, they transformed some of the city's large swamps—old properties, then considered unhealthy and too humid but which the company acquired from private landowners—into São Paulo's most luxurious districts. In these new urbanized neighborhoods, mostly conceived for the upper and upper-middle classes, the concept of the garden city was introduced for the first time in South America. As part of its strategy of urbanization, which was highly supported by São Paulo's government, the British company also provided essential complementary services, such as electricity and transportation.

Working for the Cia City, in 1913, the renowned English architect Barry Parker designed *Jardim América,* São Paulo's very first *bairro jardim,* or "garden district," not as a residential neighborhood but as a "closed community."[8] In 1917, the architect redesigned *Jardim América's* layout, transforming its division of huge lots into a strictly residential one, punctuated by semi-public gardens accessible through picturesque alleys. This decision was based in the Municipal Decree of 1929, which not only prohibited the construction of non-residential buildings in this district but also established the required setbacks and alignments. The premises of the Municipal Decree established that the *bairros jardins* could be read as a prelude for the processes of social distance and enclosure that were catalyzed at the end of the twentieth century, when the metropolis started to show an upward trend in crime rates. Henceforth, fences and surveillance cameras replaced nature as an enclosing device, and São Paulo became the "city of walls" described by the anthropologist Teresa Caldeira.[9]

The development of these dispersed and yet strictly urbanized green residential "islands" took advantage of the new avenues created after Maia's *Plano de Avenidas.* The Cia City was also responsible for the opening of these avenues, including the erstwhile Anhangabaú Avenue and today's Nove de Julho Avenue as well as its extension, in the 1930s, to the *Jardim América.* This north-south axis connecting some of the *bairros jardins* with other parts of

An aerial view of the Tamanduateí River. On the right, São Paulo's historical city center can partially be seen; on the left, some old industrial developments and administrative buildings.

Vista Aérea do Rio Tamanduateí. Na direita, o centro histórico de São Paulo pode ser visto parcialmente; na esquerda, alguns loteamentos industriais e prédios administrativos.

the city is still one of São Paulo's main avenues. Hence, if São Paulo's successive master plans were only partially followed—for example, the *Plano de Avenidas*—or never implemented, these planned urban fragments could be read as their very result: the successive master plans defined a city that is open to these kinds of private intervention that take place in the dimension of the urban lot.

And yet São Paulo's public transportation system did not accompany this accelerated process of discontinuous urban growth. Its subway, which opened in September 1974, has four lines (a fifth is still on paper) but gives no sense of the RMSP's scale. The insufficient development was the result of a shortage of financial resources, but that is no longer the case. However, the urban transportation scenario in São Paulo is marked by a massive presence of helicopters. According to *Veja* magazine, the RMSP has the largest helicopter fleet in the world outside the United States.[10] This fleet, associated with a total lack of air-traffic planning, is responsible for the fact that São Paulo has seventy times more heliports than New York City and seven times the combined number of heliports in Tokyo, Los Angeles, Frankfurt, London, Rome, Chicago, and Paris. Helicopters are certainly a more effective way to connect the urban fragments of the RMSP than any other mode of transportation, especially with regard to heavy traffic jams.

But bridging the social gap between the two extremes of the RMSP's population—helicopter users on the one hand, *peruas* users on the other—a new middle class is emerging from macroeconomic restructuring and social-assistance programs consistently implemented by recent government administrations. The social-assistance measures have lifted approximately thirty million people above Brazil's poverty line. Consequently, the internal consumer market has expanded significantly. In this new national scenario, with its numerous commercial centers, shopping malls, and other services, the RMSP represents the main destiny attracting people from all over the country and the world. In the actual global order, as of 2009, Brazil occupies a new position within the formation of the BRIC quartet of emerging powers—Brazil, Russia, India, and China—and São Paulo is definitely one of the main investment regions.

Once a large industrial city, the RMSP today is a global megacity of businesses and services. This condition is producing developments with a new mixed program, including parking, hotels, conference centers, and fashion-show venues. Former industrial areas and historic buildings, particularly those structures located in the environs of the city center, are turning into open markets, a new reality that has been accompanied by the intense process of gentrification. Since the country's political democratization in the early 1980s, members of popular housing movements, such as the *Movimento por Moradia no Centro*, or the "Movement for Housing in the City Center," tried to resist this situation. By moving into some of the vacant and derelict buildings in the city's downtown area, most people ended up being removed but not relocated, intensifying the process of exodus toward the RMPS's *periferias*.

CEU Butantã: (inaugurated in 2003), the school is located at the main building, whereas the disc-shaped building houses the kindergarten.

CEU Butantã: (inaugurada em 2003), a escola esta localizada no prédio principal, enquanto o prédio com formato de disco abriga o jardim de infância.

Indeed, this population has been pushed out to the city's peripheral settlements since the 1970s. Characterized by the absence of urban planning and by an architecture without architects, these settlements constitute the RMPS's developers of the discontinuous urban fabric. And yet, from January 2010 to December 2010, private developers launched 67,775 residential units in São Paulo, whereas in the second most important Brazilian city—Rio de Janeiro—16,787 were launched in the same period.[11] These new urban developments for the emergent middle class follow the evolution of the "closed community" tendency of the *bairros jardins* of the 1910s. They were later intensified by the real state and gated communities of the 1970s, such as Alphaville, created by the developer Albuquerque & Takaoka,[12] which the French philosopher Paul Virilio defined as a veritable "bunker for the elites."[13] Alphaville consists of highly enclosed suburban developments for both industrial and commercial ventures and for residences of the upper social classes. The community was created not only because of São Paulo's increased violence but also because of traffic and a shortage of parks.

The 1970s also marked the rise of other, similar urban developments, such as the pioneer *Condomínio Ilha do Sul*[14] (1973), located in Alto de Pinheiros and created by Albuquerque & Takaoka to be an upper-middle-class district in the west zone of São Paulo. Because of the high prices of urban real estate, *Ilha do Sul* is a vertical gated development with six towers that houses a club with one indoor and two outdoor swimming pools, a sauna, barbecue facilities, playgrounds, a library, a day-care center, a nightclub, numerous ballrooms, a piano room, and a theater where the famous Brazilian singer Elis Regina played,[15] all surrounded by green areas. This new urban typology, organized as a reinvented city within the denied city, is a heterotopia[16] that is highly controlled by security guards and cameras. It follows *Ilha do Sul's* commercial slogan: "An infrastructure turned toward leisure, comfort, and security."[17] This slogan encompasses everything that São Paulo is not.

Ilha do Sul's scheme became a paradigm for middle-class twenty-first-century residential developments as well as a symbol of the failure of the public development of cultural and sports facilities, parks, and public squares.[18] In terms of marketing and user preferences, however, the new developments are even more sophisticated today. Either inspired by the typologies of the French chateaux or Spanish villa, the architecture is rarely conceived with the participation of well-known São Paulo architects, such as the Pritzker Prize–winner Paulo Mendes da Rocha and his disciples, members of the so-called Paulista School or Paulista Brutalism.[19] If the elites embraced Brazilian Modern architecture in the 1950s, that has not been the case in the last decades. This refusal was due mostly to the absence of Joao Batista Vilanova Artigas (1915–85), considered the Paulista School's "founder" and its other exiled representatives during Brazil's dictatorship period (1964–85).

Ilha do Sul. (inaugurated in 1973).

Ilha do Sul. (inaugurado em 1973).

As a result, Paulista architects have begun to question the scope of their effective field of action and are exploring alternative strategies for reading the territory and making an impact on the built environment. Whereas real estate developers intensified the isolation of the new condos, some architects have shifted their focus from buildings to infrastructural works, emphasizing their public value and systemic character and aiming to stitch together the urban fragments.

While public programs to transform education, housing, sanitation, flooding, and water resource management are already under way in São Paulo, these architects believe they should urbanize infrastructure and expand its values. These interventions are aimed at maximizing public investments and engendering urbanity à *tout prix*. The *Centros de Educação Unificada* (CEU), or Unified Educational Centers, built by the municipality of São Paulo between 2002 and 2004, are an example. Each CEU consists of a group of sports, cultural, and education facilities spatially distributed in three prefabricated buildings, articulated by a plaza. For Alexandre Delijaicov, one of the architects responsible for the project, the acronym CEU—adopted by the mayor of São Paulo at the time—stands instead for *Centros de Estruturação Urbana*, or Centers of Urban Structuring. As Renato Anelli put it, "The CEUs want to inaugurate a new urbanity for their districts. . . . they aim at identifying the territorial situation of the area where they are established."[20] Hence, the plan was to build a network of CEUs in three phases: twenty-one in the first, another twenty-four in the second, and, to organize a special CEU, re-articulating forty-five municipal facilities in the third phase.[21]

Even though the project was interrupted due to political reasons, the extent of the intervention can be shown in the housing numbers. In the first phase, twenty-one CEUs were built, with fourteen facilities each, totaling 294 new public facilities located at the RMSP's periphery. CEU theater and sports facilities were also meant to serve the public schools and high schools situated in their environs. But the CEUs aimed at structuring not only the surrounding facilities but also the city itself: in every site where a CEU was implemented, the architects involved tried to design the surrounding streets, often unpaved, providing new street furniture—such as benches, lighting, and bridges for streams—and organizing both landscape and waterscape. As opposed to Prestes Maia's premises adopted in São Paulo during the 1930s, Delijaicov is a strong advocate of the RMSP's waterscape and of the navigability of its rivers and streams[22] Therefore, the CEU was used as a parameter for intervention at the metropolitan scale with the purpose of providing education, infrastructure, and urbanity for the RMPS's poorest regions. The architect MMBB's "Watery Voids" and "Antonico Creek" urban projects are two other examples of interventions of the same kind.[23]

In order to confront the floods, the state has built *piscinões,* which are giant basins that catch the excess water. Of the 131 *piscinões* planned to hold 15.5 million cubic meters of water, forty-two have now been completed. For most of the year, the basins are no more than immense open holes in the middle of the city. MMBB Arquitetos, an

Top: An aerial view of Paraisopolis and MMBB's "Antonico Creek" urban project, 2008.
Bottom left: MMBB's "Watery Voids" (2007).
Bottom right: MMBB's "Antonico Creek" urban project, 2008.
Acima: Vista aérea do Paraisópolis e MMBB's "Antonico Creek" projeto urbano, 2008.
Abaixo Esquerda: MMBB's "Watery Voids" (2007).
Abaixo Direita: MMBB's " Antonico Creek" projeto urbano, 2008.

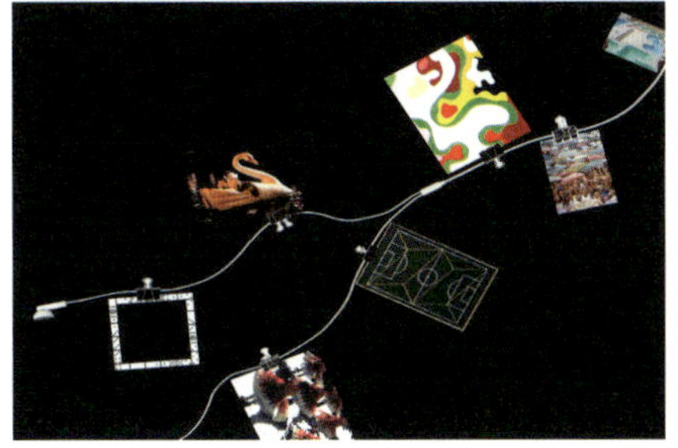

architecture practice based in São Paulo led by architects Fernando de Mello Franco, Marta Moreira, and Milton Braga, hypothesizes that the emergence of a new social class in the RMSP provides an opportunity to investigate new demands for the city's urbanity. With the "Watery Voids" project, MMBB calls for abandoning the exclusively technical view of infrastructure works. Thus, the architect has proposed the redesign of the hydrographical system in such a way that it creates a structuring system on the periphery, creating a new network of public spaces that can strengthen social bonds in this metropolis. For most of the year, the basins can serve as playgrounds, football fields, skating parks, or gathering spots. Similar to Debord's psychogeographic maps, the diagram MMBB's designed for "Watery Voids" shows that the architect is interested not only in the program fragments but also in the connective network of urban voids.

MMBB's "Antonico Creek" urban project is part of the *favelas* urbanization program undertaken by the Municipal Housing Secretary of São Paulo. The site is located in Paraisópolis, the city's second-largest *favela,* which emerged from the failure of a previous urban project; it has an area of about one square kilometer, or 0.386 square miles, and about 60,000 inhabitants. The creek cuts through an orthogonal grid that was irresponsibly built on a highly irregular topography. The design project consists of a new drainage system and the reconfiguration of open spaces. Fernando de Mello Franco noted, "The project will create a linear spine comprising a sequence of public spaces, similar to one of the most powerful spatial structures in Brazilian cities: the *calçadão*—that is, a paved corridor is often employed to make the transition between a beach and the urban fabric."[24]

For MMBB, the presence of a body of water with which one could interact in the context of Paraisópolis would salute an imaginary beach culture. MMBB defines this beach culture as the "spontaneous use of space that culturally allows for an active and desirable co-existence, though not totally devoid of conflict."[25]

To give a better understanding of why architects such as MMBB, Alexandre Delijaicov and Mendes da Rocha are fond of water, rivers, beaches and boats, relates back to Foucault's explanation of why the boat has not only been the great instrument of economic development, but also the greatest reserve of the imagination. "The ship is the heterotopia par excellence. In civilizations without boats, dreams dry up, espionage takes the place of adventure, and the police take the place of pirates."[26]

Will architects and users in the RMSP be able to rely less on police and security guards and more on boats? Able or not, these projects indicate a field for potential investigation. Indeed the shifting challenges of infrastructure and residential development in a burgeoning metropolis such as the RMSP could serve as an appropriate inspiration for a new search of mental mapping and thus programming at the level of an architecture studio.

I gratefully acknowledge Tal Schori, Noah Biklen, Nina Rappaport, Márcio Grossman, Marcos Leite Rosa, Anna Gomes, Nelson Kon, Milton Braga, Fernando de Mello Franco, Guilherme Pianca, Alexandre Delijaicov, Andre Takiya, Wanderley Ariza, Richard Scoffier and Jean-Louis Violeau for their input and help.

1 Guy-Ernest Debord, "Introduction à une critique de la géographie urbaine" in *Les Lèvres nues* no. 6, September 1955.

2 Leandro Medrano, Luiz Recamán, "Espaços públicos na região central da cidade de São Paulo: O Telecentro Elevado Costa e Silva" in: Vitruvius arquitextos, 2006, n. 075. Editorial, August 2006, p.1 available in: <http://www.vitruvius.com.br/revistas/read/arquitextos/07.075/326> (Last access on May 22, 2011).

3 The RMSP was created that year through a Federal Law, subsequently institutionalized by a State Law and finally implemented in 1975.

4 Website of Emplasa, Data from 2006: <http://www.emplasa.sp.gov.br> (Last access on May 23, 2011).

5 Otília Arantes, Carlos Vainer, Ermínia Maricato. *A cidade do pensamento único: desmanchando consensos.* Petrópolis: Vozes, 2000.

6 For more on this process, see: Mariana Fix. *Parceiros da Exclusão: duas histórias da construção de uma "nova cidade" em São Paulo: Faria Lima e Agua Espraiada.* São Paulo: Boitempo, 2001.

7 Website of Cia City: <http://www.ciacity.com.br> (Last access on May 21, 2011).

8 Teresa Caldeira, *City of Walls: Crime, Segregation, and Citizenship in São Paulo.* Berkeley: University of California Press, 2001.

9 *Veja* (March 13, 2002): 70.

10 João Crestana and Celso Petrucci, "Consolidação das pesquisas do mercado imobiliário," Câmara Brasileira da Indústria da Construção (2011).

11 Albuquerque & Takaoka is an architecture, civil engineering and real estate development private company. This São Paulo-based firm founded in 1951 by two young civil engineers, Renato de Albuquerque and Yojiro Takaoka, who were colleagues and graduated together in 1949, in the course at the *Escola Politécnica da Universidade de São Paulo* (Polytechnic School).

12 Paul Virilio, "A catástrofe urbana," *Folha de São Paulo*, Caderno Mais! (Interview). São Paulo, August 24, 1997.

13 Website of Ilha do Sul: <http://www.ilhadosul.com.br> (Last accessed on May 21, 2011).

14 Ibid.

15 According to Michel Foucault's sixth principle of "Heterotopias," the role of the latter is "to create a space that is other, another real space, as perfect, as meticulous, as well arranged as ours is messy, ill constructed, and jumbled. This latter type would be the heterotopia, not of illusion, but of compensation." See: Michel Foucault, "Dits et écrits 1984, Des espaces autres" (Conference at the Cercle d'études architecturales, March 14,1967), published in *Architecture, Mouvement, Continuité*, n.5 (October 1984): pp. 46-49.

16 Ibid.

17 And yet in 1989 *Alto de Pinheiros* gained a park, extremely close to *Ilha do Sul.* The Villa-Lobos Park, with its 750 square meters of green area, was built on the former site of a waste deposit for the material dredged from the Pinheiros River, where eighty families used to live and work in garbage collection. The families were removed, and *Ilha do Sul's* residents have now two leisure options: their private club and the park. But that is not the reality of the great majority of the RMSP's population, who live far from the very few city parks.

18 For more on the Paulista School, see Ruth Verde Zein. *A arquitetura da escola paulista brutalista:* 1953-1973. Ph.D. diss. Rio Grande to Sul Federal University, Porto Alegre, 2007.

19 Renato Anelli, "Centros Educacionais Unificados: arquitetura e educaçãoo em São Paulo" in: Vitruvius arquitextos, 2004, N. 055.0 2. December 2004, p.2 available in: <http://www.vitruvius.com.br/arquitextos/arq055/arq055_02.asp>

20 Marisa Pulice Mascarenhas; Patricia Salomãoo, (Fundação Instituto de Administração), Recordings of an interview with Alexandre Delijaicov, Andre Takiya, Wanderley Ariza and Rosana Miranda - CEU, São Paulo 2004.

21 Delijaicov's Ph.d. dissertation defended in 2005 is dedicated to this topic. See: Alexandre Delijaicov, *São Paulo, metrópole fluvial: os rios e a arquitetura da cidade. Parques e portos fluviais urbanos: projeto da cidade-canal Billings-Taiaçupeba.* Ph.D. diss. University of São Paulo, São Paulo, 2005.

22 MMBB is an architecture practice based in São Paulo, led by architects Fernando de Mello Franco, Marta Moreira and Milton Braga. The office has been working in informal areas since 2007 when it received the Best Entry Award at the 3rd International Architecture Biennale in Rotterdam for its Watery Voids project.

23 MMBB's website: <http:// mmbb.com.br/> (Last access on May 21, 2011).

24 Ibid.

25 Foucault, op. cit.

26 Michel Foucault, "Of Other Spaces" in *Diacritics*, Vol. 16, n.1 (Spring 1986): 27.

III. URBAN SECTIONS WORK AT

III. INTERSECÇÕES URBANAS: TRABALHO EM ESTUDIO NA UNIVERSIDADE YALE

INTER-
: STUDIO
YALE

BEM-VINDO A SÃO PAULO

BEM VINDO A SÃO PAULO

Opposite: Vilanova Artigas, architect, Edificio Louveira, São Paulo, 1946–49.
Oposto: Vilanova Artigas, arquiteto, Edifício Louveira, São Paulo, 1946–49.

São Paulo has grown rapidly over the past one hundred years to a density of 9,000 people per square kilometer and a population of over 17 million.[1] Layers of urban experiments, development, and auto-construction have resulted in a vibrant, multi-centered city characterized by disjunction. São Paulo is a "city of walls," according to anthropologist Teresa Caldeira, yet the processes of social distance and enclosure have coincided with political democratization, the growth of social movements, and multivalent efforts to establish services for the informal spaces of the city.[2]

While much critical attention has been paid to how São Paulo's urban poor and extremely affluent engage the formal and informal built environment, this studio focused on the emerging middle-class inhabitants of the city. Between 2004 and 2008, the middle class in Brasil increased by 10 percent. Combined with social programs such as "Bolsa Familia" to combat both extreme poverty and inequality and a 100 percent increase in the minimum wage during the past decade, the recent rise of the middle class has profound implications for the city's urban spaces of consumption and housing markets, both formal and informal.[3] The Instituto Brasileiro de Geografia e Estatística estimates there is a deficit of approximately eight million housing units in Brazil, ranging from low- to upper-income housing.

A new middle-class mixed-use development on a 181,000-square-meter site, adjacent to the Marginal Tietê Highway and the Tietê River in São Paulo, is complex in both its peripheral disposition to the urban center and the requirements set by the developer, Tishman Speyer. Zoning allows for 325,000 square meters of residential, retail, and commercial development. Access to the site, existing aboveground high-power lines, and several historic buildings provide planning and development complexities, as does necessary project phasing.

The students were asked to approach the project from the perspective of both the designer and developer and to engage issues of schedule, risk, flexibility, value, and rates of return, along with scale, formal clarity, envelope articulation, environmental sensitivity and climate, use of color and texture and the relationship of building to landscape. We asked, what are the possibilities for creating a new urban space that is both secure and accessible? How does the project distribute the density and parking requirements assumed by the developer's initial pro forma on a site whose immediate context has a much lower density? The resulting projects investigated new approaches to shared public space and access within a private development. They integrated sustainable practices of natural ventilation, shading, and the alleviation of seasonal flooding while considering inventive architectural forms for dense housing and mixed-use programs to connect an isolated site with the larger city.

1 http://www.citymayors.com/statistics/largest-cities-density-125.html

2 Teresa Caldeira, *City of Walls: Crime, Segregation, and Citizenship in São Paulo*. Berkeley: University of California Press, 2000.

3 See Perry Anderson, "Lula's Brazil," *London Review of Books*, vol. 33 No. 7 (31 March 2011), pages 3-12, and *The Economist*, "A Better Today: Brazil's Growing Middle Class Wants The Good Life, Right Now," (12 November 2009), http://www.economist.com/node/14829501.

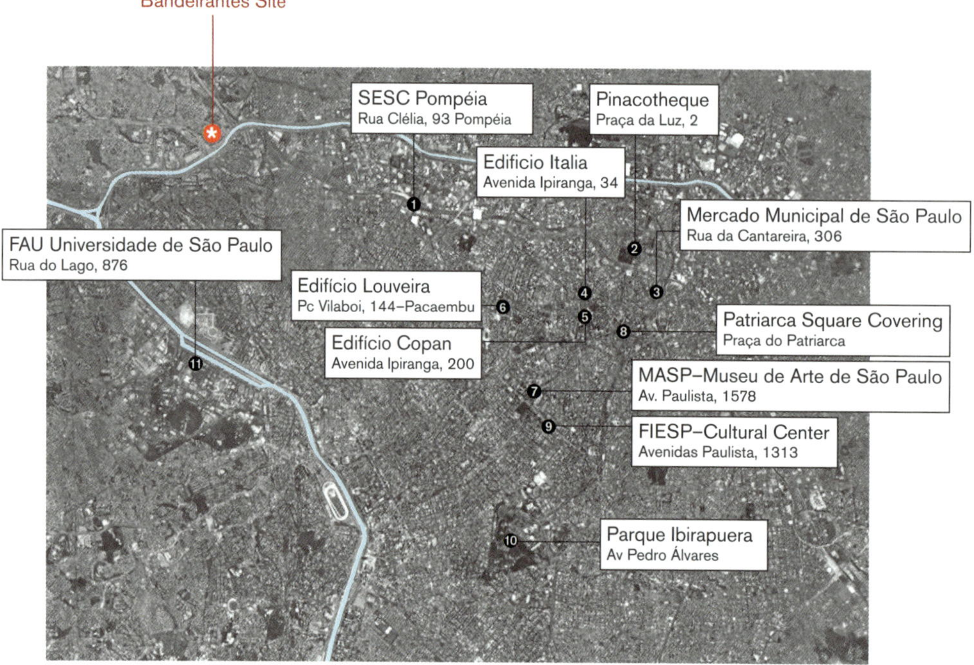
Bandeirantes Site
SESC Pompéia
Rua Clélia, 93 Pompéia
Pinacotheque
Praça da Luz, 2
Edificio Italia
Avenida Ipiranga, 34
Mercado Municipal de São Paulo
Rua da Cantareira, 306
FAU Universidade de São Paulo
Rua do Lago, 876
Edifício Louveira
Pc Vilaboi, 144–Pacaembu
Edifício Copan
Avenida Ipiranga, 200
Patriarca Square Covering
Praça do Patriarca
MASP–Museu de Arte de São Paulo
Av. Paulista, 1578
FIESP–Cultural Center
Avenidas Paulista, 1313
Parque Ibirapuera
Av Pedro Álvares

Vilanova Artigas, architect, A Faculdade de Arquitetura e Urbanismo da Universidade de São Paulo, São Paulo, 1961–68.
Opposite top: Key Plan
Opposite bottom: Paulo Mendes da Rocha, architect, Patriarca Square Covering, São Paulo, 1992.

Vilanova Artigas, arquiteto, A Faculdade de Arquitetura e Urbanismo da Universidade de São Paulo, São Paulo, 1961-68.
Oposto acima: Plano Chave
Oposto abaixo: Paulo Mendes da Rocha, arquiteto, Praca do Patriarca, São Paulo, 1992.

Lina Bo Bardi, architect, SESC Pompéia, São Paulo, 1977–78.
Opposite: Oscar Niemeyer, architect, Auditorium in Ibirapuera, São Paulo 2002–05.
Lina Bo Bardi, arquiteta, SESC Pompeia, São Paulo, 1977–78.
Oposto: Oscar Niemeyer, arquiteto, Auditorio do Ibirapuera, São Paulo, 2002–05.

CIRCOLO ITALIAN

Lina Bo Bardi, architect, MASP-Modern Art Museum of São Paulo, São Paulo, 1957.
Opposite, clockwise from top left: Adolf Franz Heep, architect, Itália Building, São Paulo, 1956.
Ramos de Azevedo and Domiziano Rossi for São Paulo Arts and Craft Lyceum at Luz Gardens, São Paulo State Pinacotheque, São Paulo, 1897. Remodeled by Paulo Mendes da Rocha, Eduardo Colonelli and Welington Torres, architects, 1993–98.
Ramos de Azevedo, architect, Public Market, São Paulo, 1926–32. Remodeled by Pedro Paulo de Mello Saraiva, architect, 2004.
Luis Roberto Carvalho Franco architects, FIESP-Cultural Center, São Paulo, 1969. Extension designed Paulo Mendes da Rocha, architect, 1996.
Lina Bo Bardi, arquiteta, MASP-Museu de Arte Moderna de São Paulo, São Paulo, 1957.
Oposto, no sentido horário do topo lado esquerdo: Adolf Franz Heep, arquiteto, Predio Italia, São Paulo, 1956.
Ramos de Azevedo e Domiziano Rossi pelo liceu das artes e ofícios de São Paulo nos Jardins da Luz, Pinacoteca do Estado de São Paulo, São Paulo, 1897. Remodelado por Paulo Mendes da Rocha, Eduardo Colonelli e Wellington Torres, arquitetos, 1993–98.
Ramos de Azevedo, arquiteto,Marcado Publico, São Paulo, 1926–32. Remodelado por Pedro Paulo de Melo Saraiva, arquiteto, 2004.
Luis Roberto Carvalho Franco Arquitetos, FIESP-Centro Cultural, São Paulo, 1969. Extensao desenhada por Paulo Mendes da Rocha, arquiteto, 1996.

Oscar Niemeyer, Zenon Lotufo, Helio Uchoa, and Eduardo Kneese de Mello, architects, Ibirapuera Park and Main Buildings/Pavillions, São Paulo, 1951.
Opposite: Oscar Niemeyer, and Garlos Lemos, architects, Edificio Copan, São Paulo, 1950–61.
Oscar Niemeyer, Zenon Lotufo, Helio Uchoa, e Eduardo Kneese de Mello, arquitetos, Parque do Ibirapuera e prêdios principais/Pavilhoes, São Paulo, 1951.
Oposto: Oscar Niemeyer, e Garlos Lemos, arquitetos, Edificio Copan, São Paulo, 1950–61.

Climate
Clima

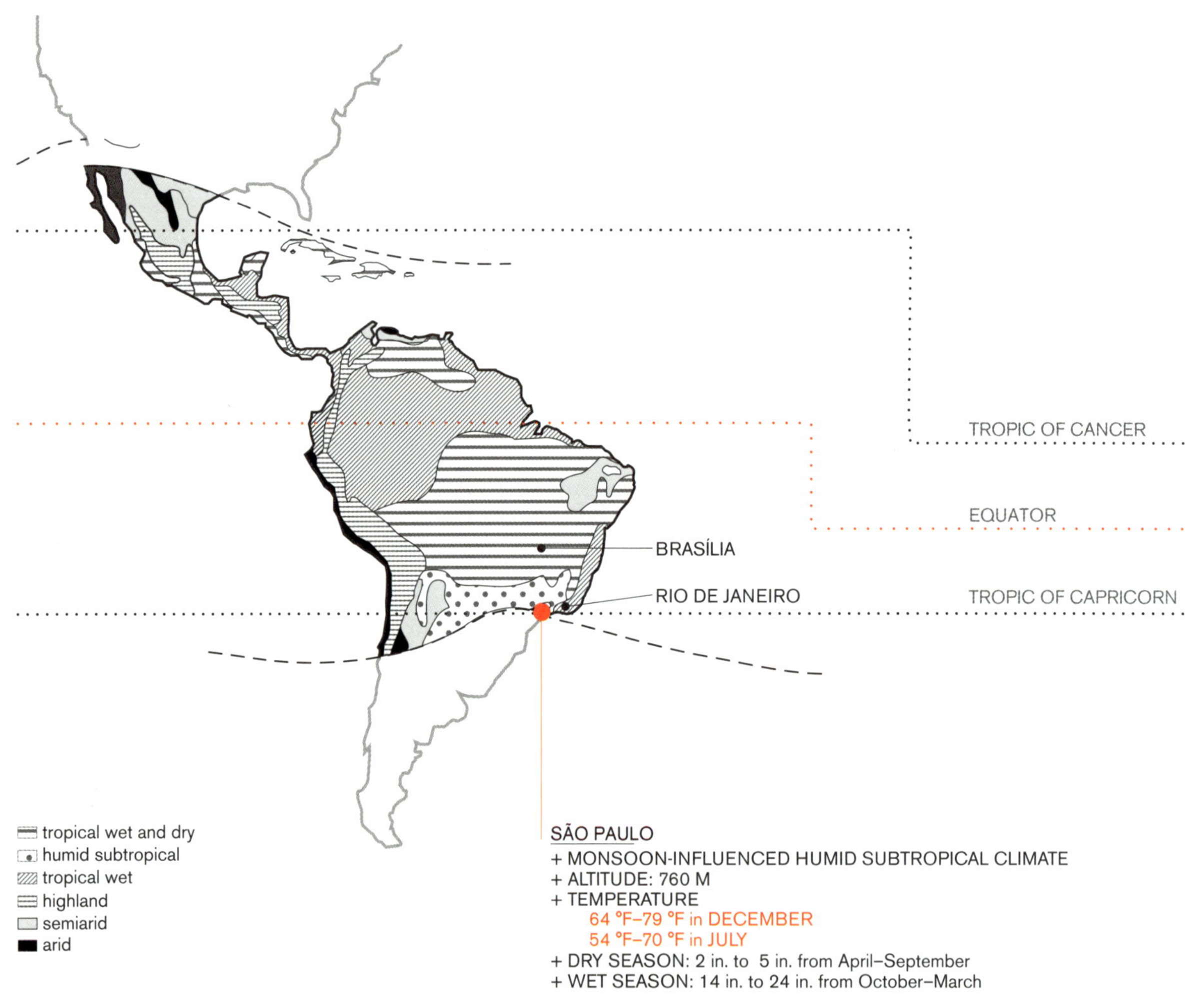

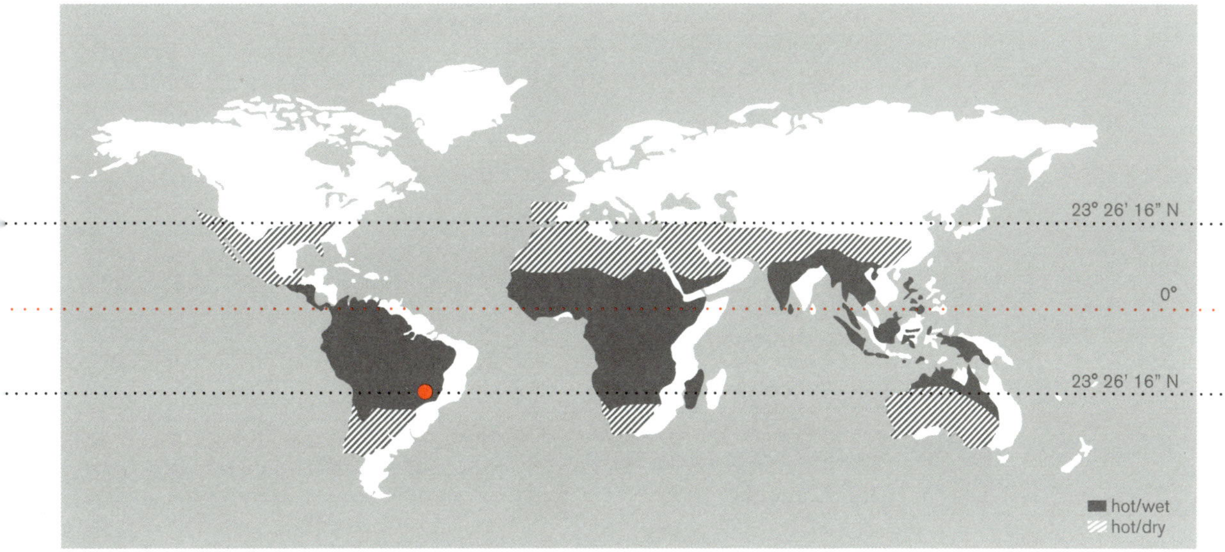

23° 26' 16" N
0°
23° 26' 16" N
hot/wet
hot/dry

INCOME

12 KM
6 KM
MINIMUM WAGE INCOME
Comparison
0.00 - 3.00
3.01 - 6.00
6.01 - 10. 00
10.01 - 14.00
14.01 - 18.00
18.01 -
Bandeirantes Site

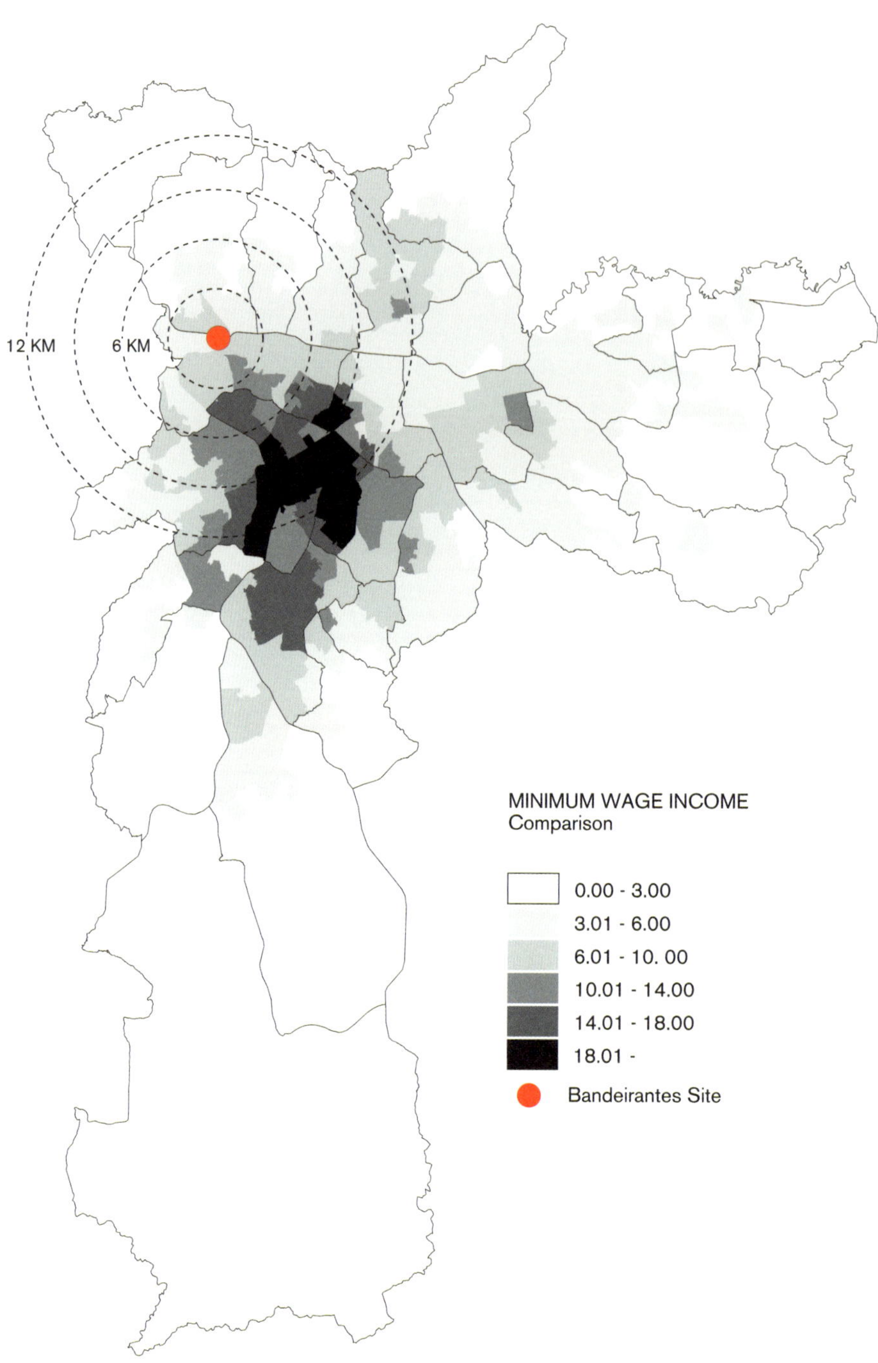

The studio was asked to research the urban growth and development in São Paulo to formulate a business approach for the programming and design of a large-scale development on the periphery of the city.

Foi pedido ao estúdio que pesquisasse o crescimento urbano e desenvolvimento em São Paulo afim de que este formulasse uma abordagem de negócios para programação e design de um empreendimento em grande escala na periferia da cidade.

RESIDENTIAL DENSITY
Horizontal Built Area

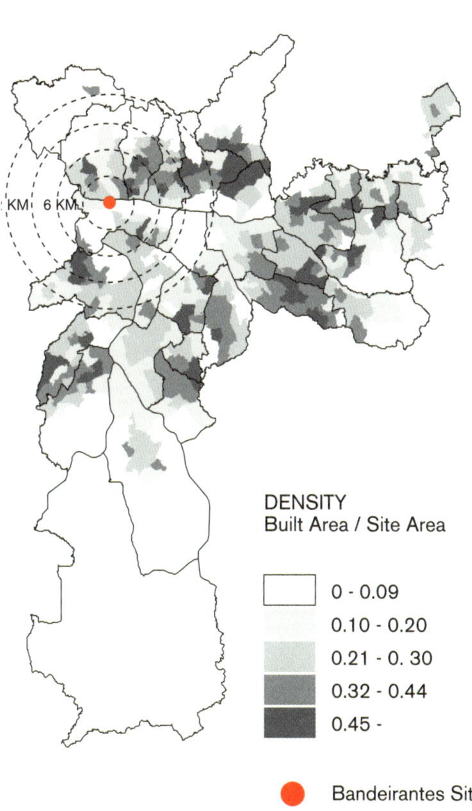

RESIDENTIAL DENSITY
Vertical Built Area

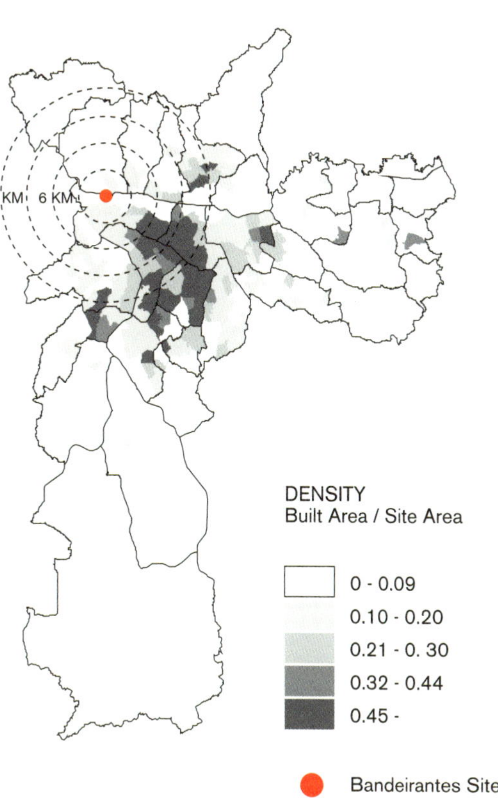

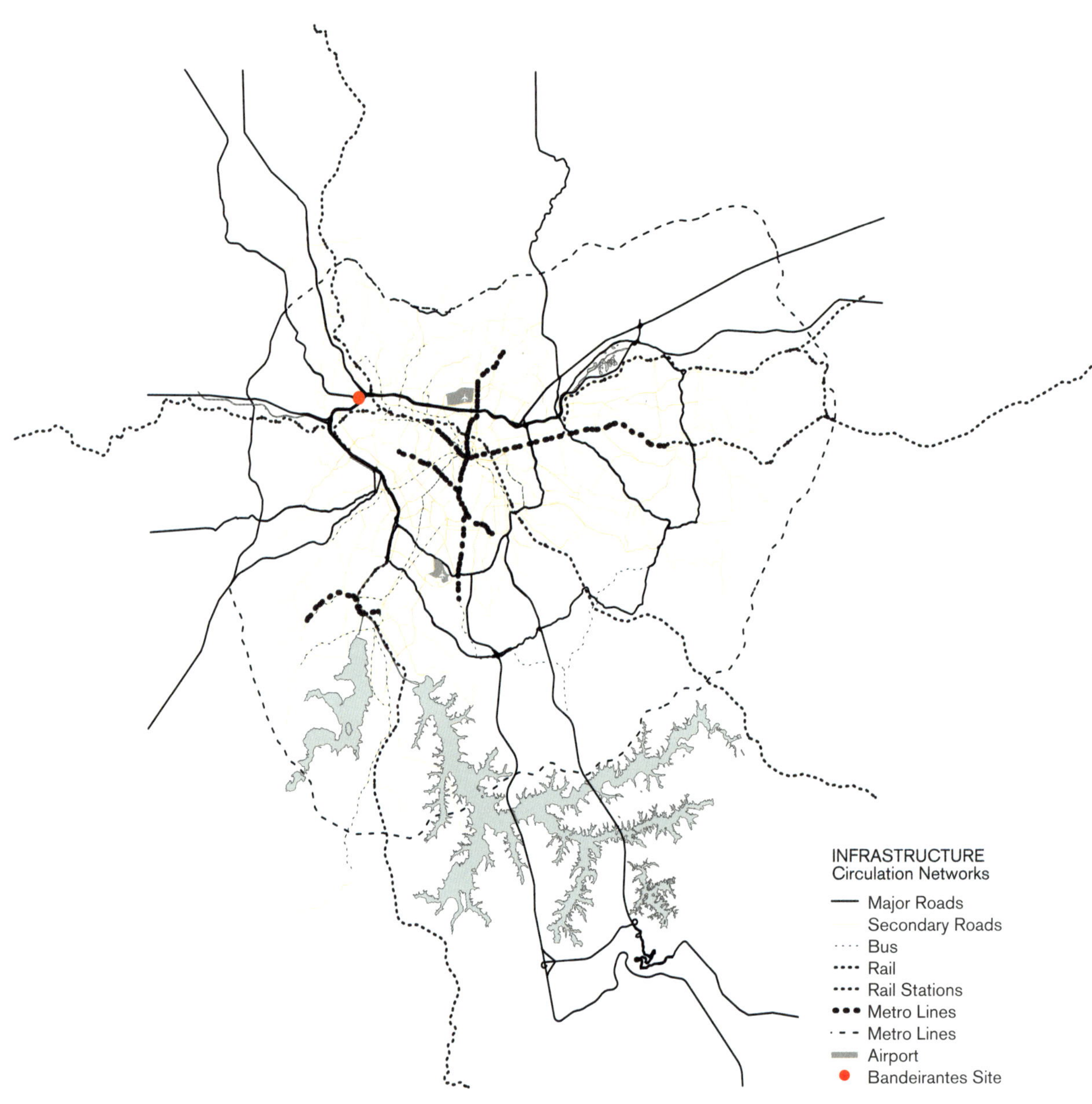
INFRASTRUCTURE
Circulation Networks
Major Roads
Secondary Roads
Bus
Rail
Rail Stations
Metro Lines
Metro Lines
Airport
Bandeirantes Site

**Landscape and Water Networks in São Paulo.
Opposite: Transportation and access are important factors in determining the feasibility of a residential mixed-use development. São Paulo's infrastructural network continues to develop but not at the speed required for the growing population.**

**Paisagem e saneamento básico em São Paulo.
Oposto: Transporte e meios de acesso são fatores importantes ao determinar a viabilidade de um empreendimento residencial de uso misto. A infra estrutura de São Paulo continua a desenvolver-se, mas não na velocidade necessária para acompanhar o crescimento da população.**

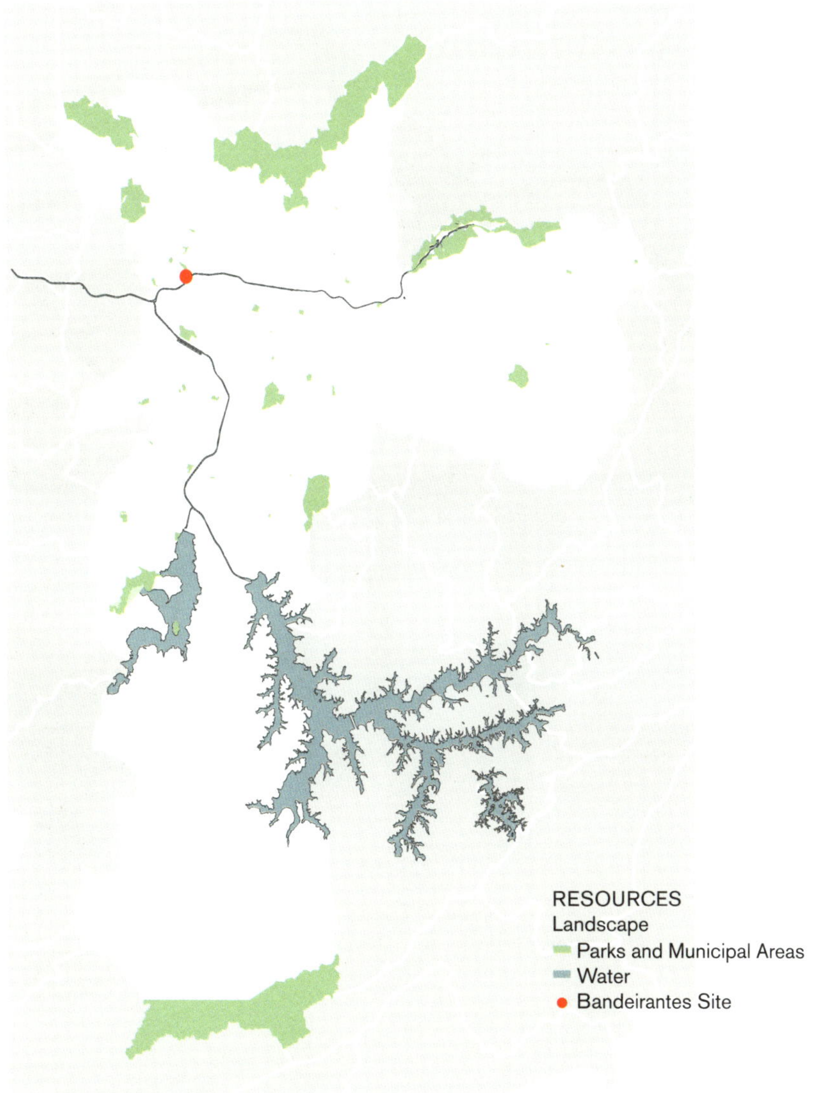

CENTER TO THE PERIPHERY: BANDEIRANTES, SÃO PAULO

DO CENTRO À PERIFERIA: BANDEIRANTES, SÃO PAULO

Opposite: Structural remnants of the Abattoir, now completely overgrown.
Oposto: Restos estruturais do Abattoir, agora completamente coberto, tem uma presença escultural.

Located six miles outside the central city, the studio's project site, Banderiantes, is isolated from its surroundings by clear physical boundaries, yet it sits at an intersection of a variety of urban uses and forms. It is surrounded by an upper-middle-class development to the west, a city park to the north, a working-class development to the east, and the highway, river, and industrial developments to the south and southwest. Aboveground power lines running along the eastern edge separate the site's upper and lower portion.

Originally operated as a farm, the site became a slaughterhouse in the early twentieth-century until 1960, when it was sold and left unused for fifty years. There are a number of manufacturing buildings that have been abandoned at the upper portion of the property, including a historic landmarked structure that used to function as a clubhouse for employees.

São Domingo, the surrounding low-rise, middle-class residential neighborhood, has a population of approximately 168,000 residents and is markedly less dense than both the adjacent areas and the density required in the developer's early studies. The initial pro forma called for about 2,500 residential units and supporting programs to sustain a new community. The developer, Tishman Speyer, explored multiple scenarios, including residential, office, and retail programs. In the most drastic scenario, the lower portion of the site would be sold to a retail operator for a shopping center.

In a city marked by extreme density, the site's undeveloped terrain, isolation, and the low density of the adjacent neighborhoods presented a unique challenge. The project offered an opportunity to consider how new approaches to urban design might provide alternatives to the repetitive towers dotting the skyline, incorporate sustainability as an organizing principle, and present varying degrees of access and enclosure between the city's public spaces, and the front door of a home.

Due to limited area resources, the program must provide ample space for neighborhood amenities and institutions.
Opposite top: The 190,000-square-meter site is one of the last of this scale remaining undeveloped in São Paulo.
Opposite bottom: The site's prime location on the Marginal Tietê has been considered by a number of retail developers as the future location for a designation shopping center.

Devido aos recursos de área limitada, o programa deve fornecer um amplo espaço para amenidades do bairro e das instituições.
Oposto acima: Os 190.000-metros-quadrados do projeto é um dos últimos desta escala que permaneceram subdesenvolvidos em São Paulo.
Oposto parte inferior: A localização privilegiada do projeto na Marginal Tietê tem sido considerada por grande número de empreendedores comerciais como a futura localização de shopping center já designado.

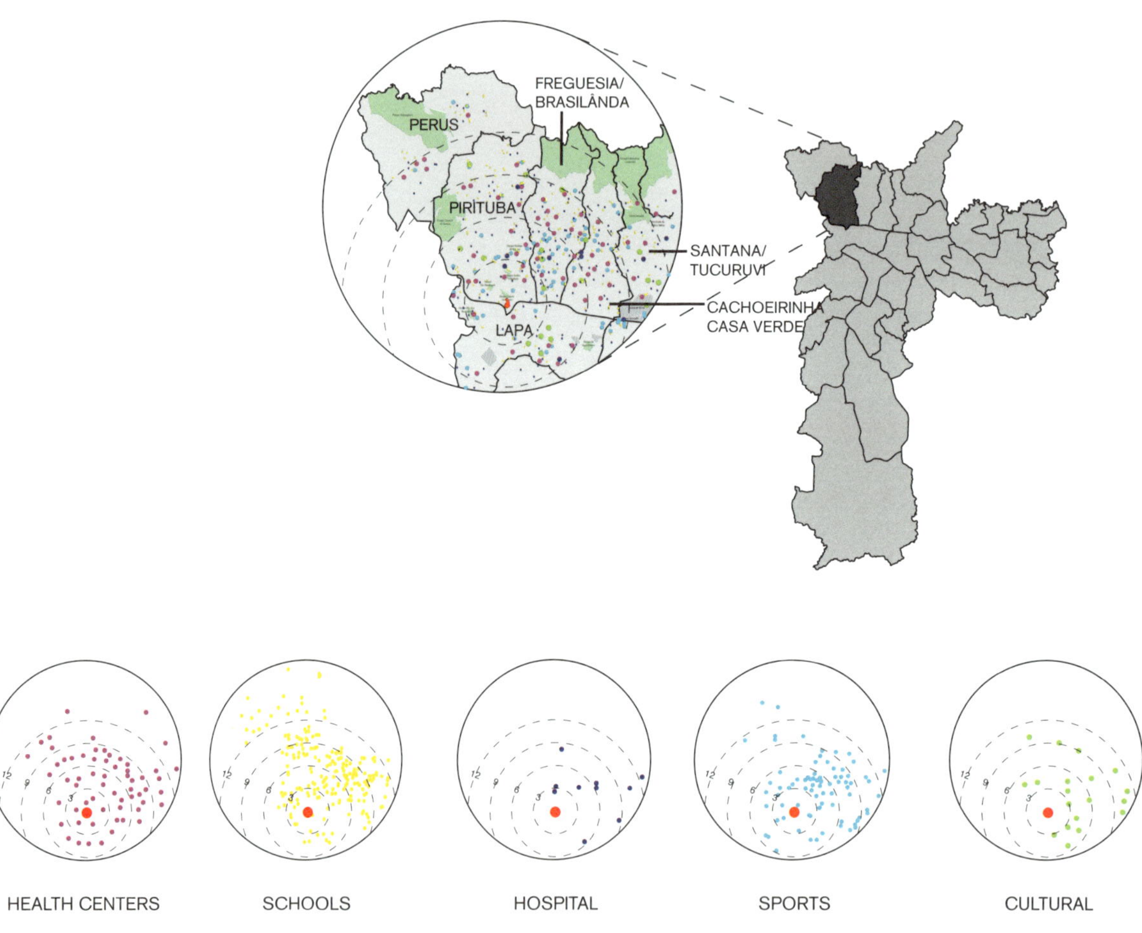

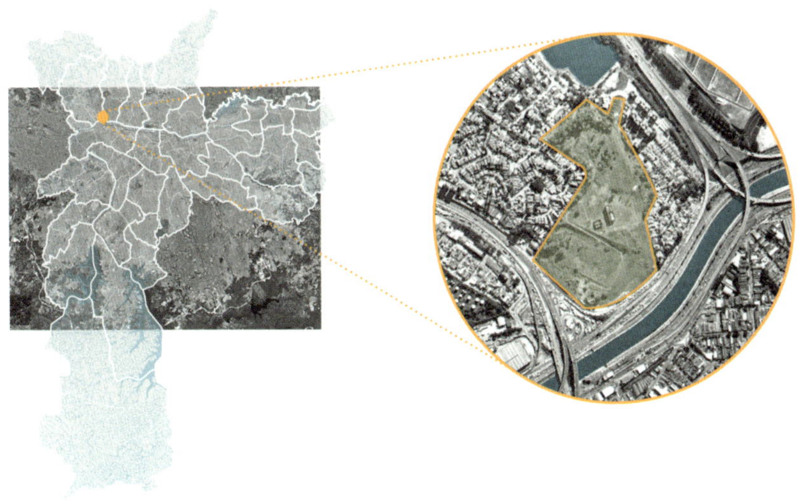

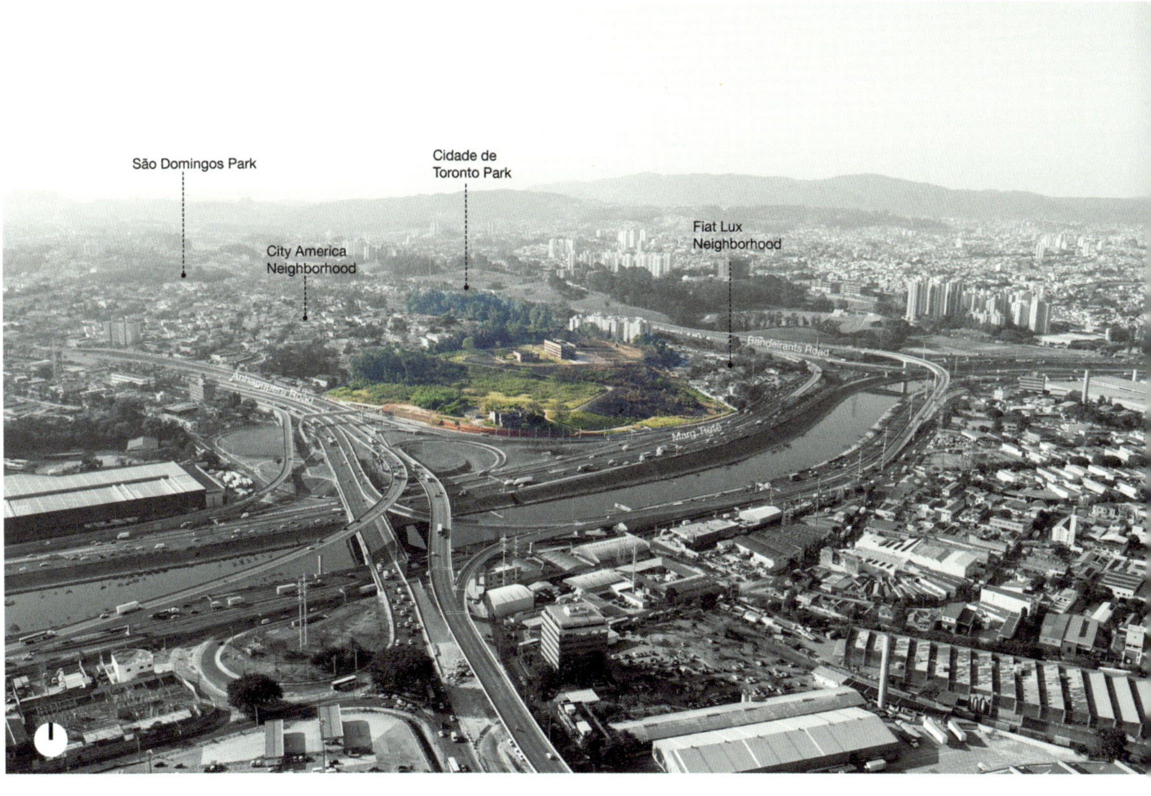

São Domingos Park
Cidade de Toronto Park
City America Neighborhood
Fiat Lux Neighborhood
Bandeirants Road
Anhanguera Road
Marg. Tietê

Panoramic view to the southeast, underneath the power lines. The Marginal Tietê highway creates a clear separation between the development site and the city.
Vista panorâmica do sudeste, abaixo dos fios de eletricidade. A auto-estrada da marginal Tietê cria uma clara separação entre o local do loteamento e a cidade.

Site Constraints and Opportunities.
Opposite: Selected precedents were placed on the site to test scale, density, and program distribution.
Restrições e oportunidades do projeto.
Oposto: Precedentes selecionados foram colocados no local para teste de densidade,escala, e distribuição do programa.

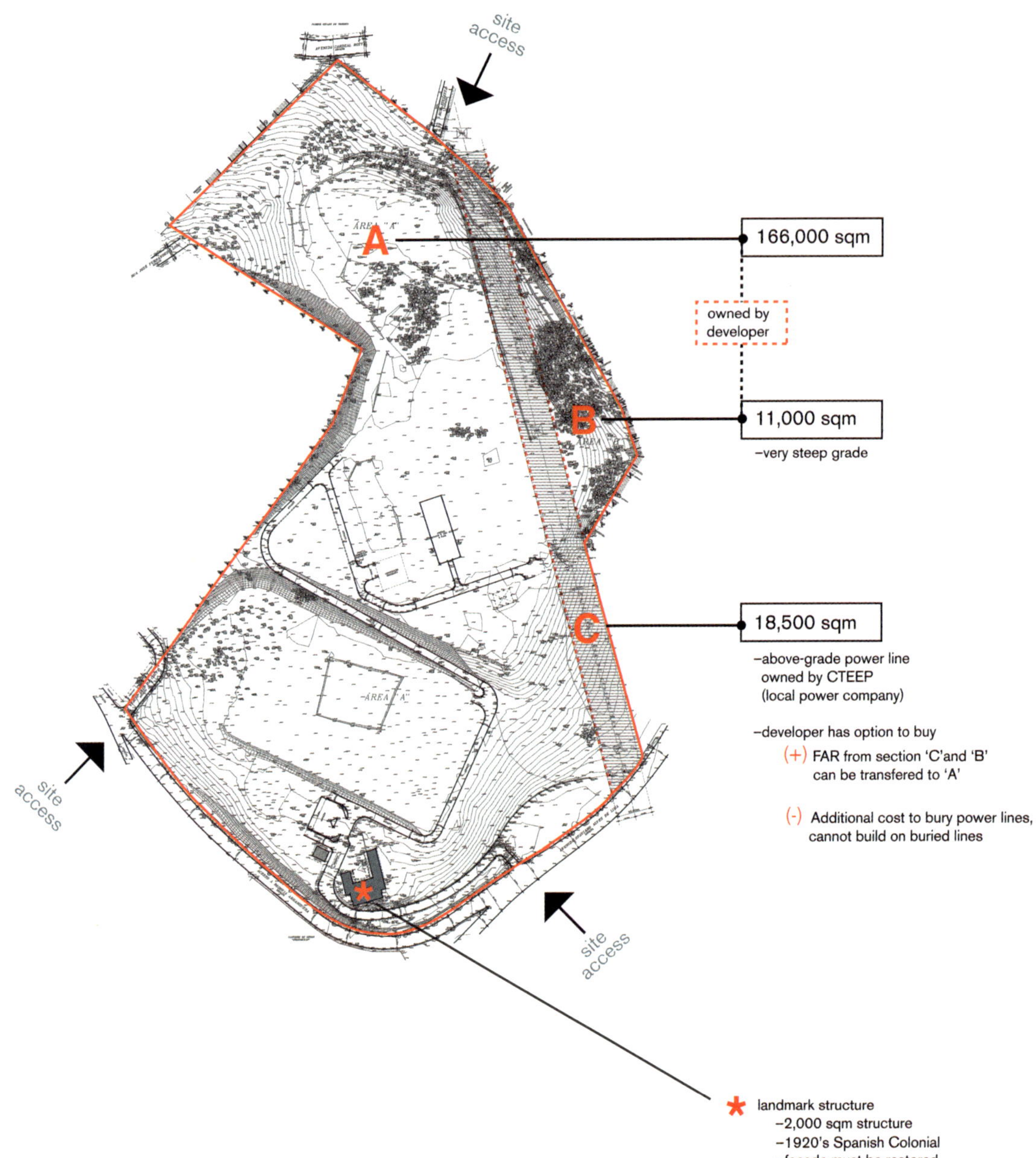

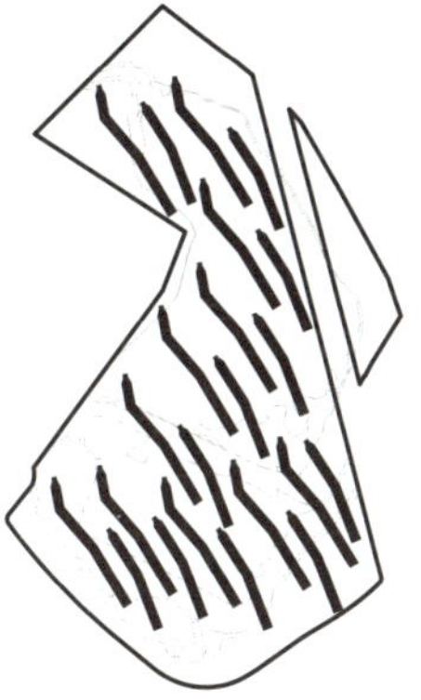

ROBIN HOOD GARDENS
Alison and Peter Smithson
London, England
1969–1972

– 2 buildings
– 213 units (total)
– 10 floors, 7 floors

ON SITE: x10 = 2,130 units

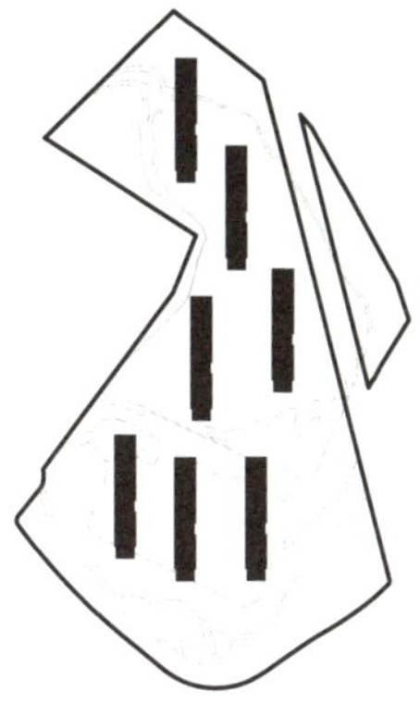

UNITÉ D'HABITATION
Le Corbusier
Marseilles, Frances
1947–1952

– 337 units
– 12 floors

ON SITE: x7 = 2,359 units

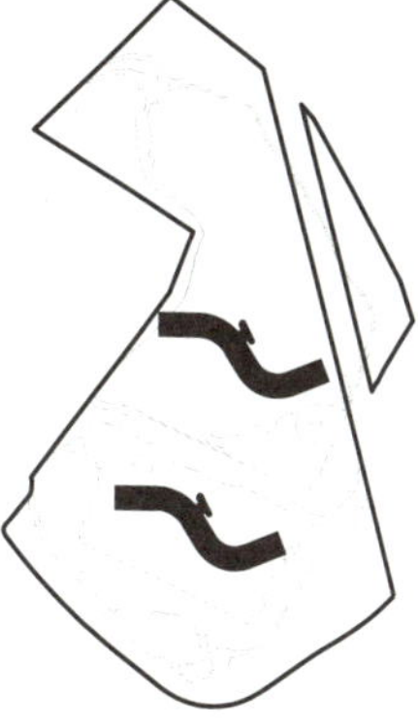

EDIFÍCIO COPAN
Oscar Niemeyer
Sao Paulo
1957–1966

– 1160 units
– 38 floors

ON SITE: x2 = 2,320 units

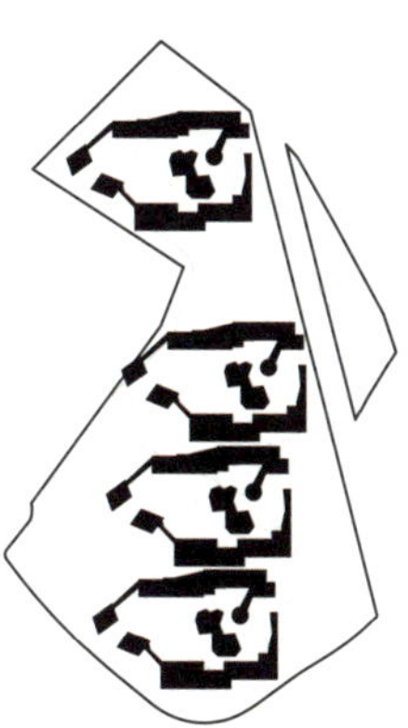

LINKED HYBRID
Steven Holl
Beijing, China
2003–2009

– 644 units
– Mixed Use

ON SITE: x4 = 2,576 units

BEEKMAN TOWER
Frank Gehry
New York, NY
2006–2010

– 903 units
– 76 floors
– Mixed Use

ON SITE: x3 = 2,709 units

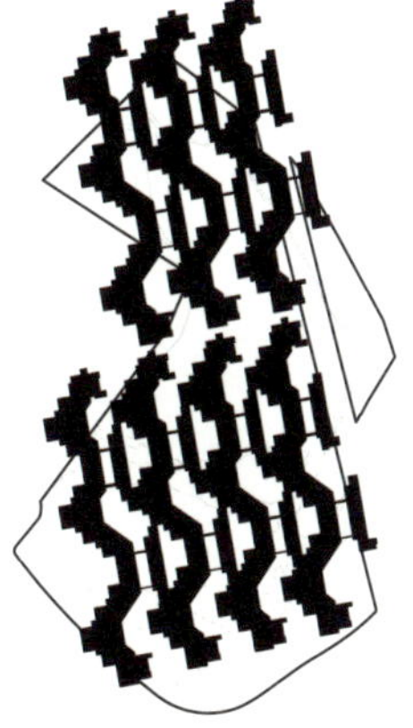

HABITAT '67
Moshe Safdie
Montreal, Canada
1967

– 158 units
– Varies

ON SITE: x7 = 1,106 units

São Paulo studio site.
Terreno do Studio São Paulo

PROJECTS

PROJETOS

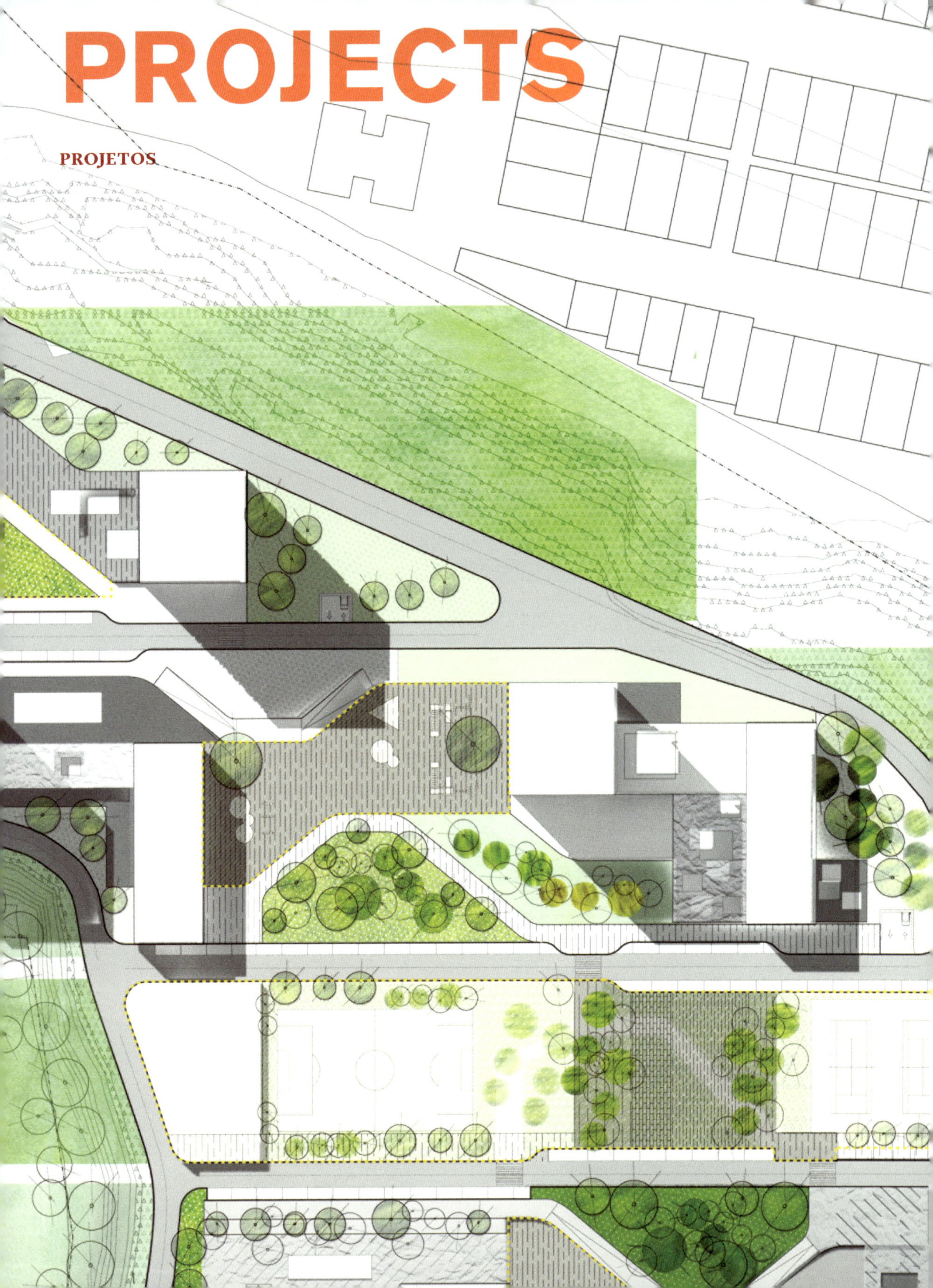

Studio Brief The studio began with a crash course in real estate concepts and São Paulo development with Nate Shanok of Tishman Speyer. He provided an overview of the tools Tishman Speyer uses to analyze the residential and commercial markets, including extensive market research and development scenario models. He also reviewed a number of scenarios for the project site, giving the students an understanding of the impact of different unit sizes, mixes of residential, retail, and commercial programs, subdivisions, phasing, and infrastructural approaches to the zoning envelope.

In the first assignment, students were asked to contextualize the conversation currently taking place among planners, developers, designers, officials, activists, and residents about the concept behind and direction for São Paulo's urban spaces and architecture. In groups of two, they gave presentations about these urban issues, touching upon infrastructure, demographics, climate, construction practices, and economic and cultural production.

They also conducted research of the mid-twentieth-century projects by Brazilian architects Oscar Niemeyer, Lina Bo Bardi, Paulo Mendes da Rocha, and João Vilanova Artigas, as well as landscape designer Roberto Burle Marx. In particular, the students were asked to consider the architects' use of form and massing, color and materials, façade techniques, site plan, and landscape strategies, all of which informed the students' scaled drawings and analytic studies of residential precedents.

In the next phase, the students quickly developed three scenarios highlighting their approach and strategy for a site plan, representing the plan with an aerial drawing or with models and a perspective drawing. Then, they prepared an initial master plan.

On their weeklong trip to Brazil they presented their concepts to the development team and met with architects, planners, and scholars working in São Paulo. They visited development projects by Tishman Speyer and toured São Paulo, Brasília, and Rio de Janeiro to see the work of the Brazilian architects whom they had studied.

After the midterm, the students shifted their focus from the scale of the master plan to the specific project site, which comprised individual residential buildings and their surrounding open spaces. In the second half of the semester, the students each developed their design at multiple scales, with particular emphasis on the integration and layering of public and semi-private spaces. The work addressed the degrees of enclosure and the articulation of exterior horizontal and vertical surfaces: building façades, landscape, and the transitional spaces between the city and the interior spaces.

Opposite: A loose grid organizes the layout of the 2,200-unit residential development; the repurposed arts buildings at the center of the site sets up an alternate geometry that subtly inflects the surrounding housing.
Oposto: Uma grade solta organiza o layout das 2, 200 unidades do loteamento residencial; os prédios de arte no centro do local criam uma geometria alternativa que sutilmente inflectem àsresidencias ao redor.

BANDEIRANTES ARTS DISTRICT Rebecca Garnett

The Bandeirantes Arts District proposes an unconventional development model to capitalize on the site's constraints by creating a new arts precinct, thereby positioning Brazil's thriving arts culture at the heart of the development. Once used as an abattoir, the ruinlike, sky-lit structures at the center of the expansive site are recast as an arts and community center similar to SESC Pompéia—a successful arts and recreation development in São Paulo made famous by the architecture of Lina Bo Bardi. The long-span industrial spaces are ideal for flexible art display configurations and act as a cultural and economic engine for this peripherally located development. Around this public arts square, a loose grid of walkable and multi-scaled fabric breaks down the 2,200-unit residential development into smaller neighborhoods. Three scales of housing are deployed according to the varied topographic and landscape conditions they inhabit; each scale is then skewered by a cultural spine comprising retail spaces, artist housing, and community recreation facilities.

Three hundred and ninety units of terraced housing negotiate twelve meters of natural grade on the south edge, taking advantage of views across the river toward the city skyline. At the middle of the site, six hundred units of mid-rise housing are laid out on the flat plateau and provide a physical connection to the adjacent residential neighborhoods. Harking back to the so-called superblocks of Brasília, the buildings on these semi-private blocks are lifted above the ground to create a sense of transparency and connectedness at the ground level. Accessible to neighborhood residents, shared amenities occur just below and above the ground plane; sunken garden courts and recreation facilities occur at the lower level, and gathering platforms are lifted just above. Thin mid-rise buildings shade the ground below and provide maximum ventilation for the units above; façades are outfitted with orientation-appropriate screens to mitigate harsh sun angles while allowing for proper ventilation. Finally, high-rise buildings with small footprints and columnar structures are positioned on the steep, wooded slopes to the north, positioned to take advantage of the expansive and expensive views of São Paulo beyond. Like the mid-rise neighborhood, these units pair well with the adjacent existing towers and share convenient access to a park at the northern edge.

This proposal calls into question the prevailing and ubiquitous use of the high-rise tower typology by complementing the vertical model with other, regionally appropriate types. In this way, middle-class residents of São Paulo are provided with a variety of urban lifestyles well outside of the city center.

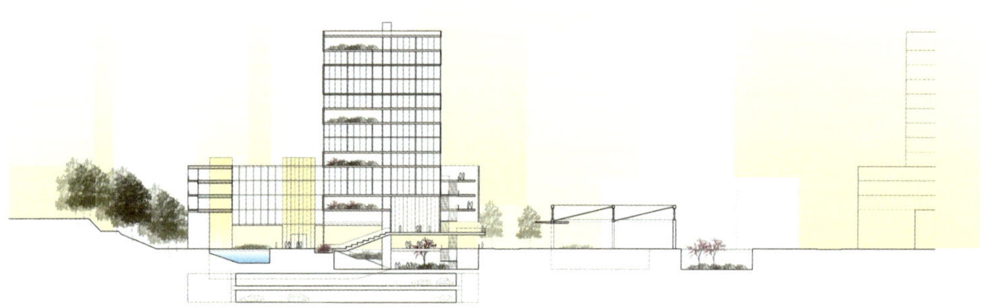

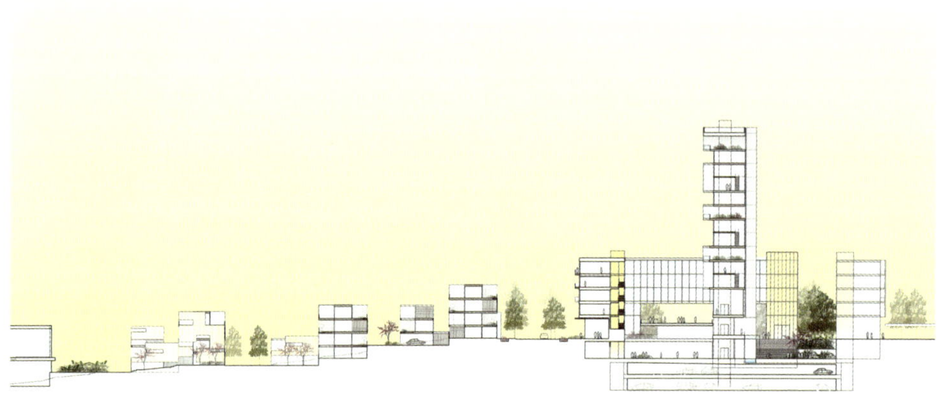

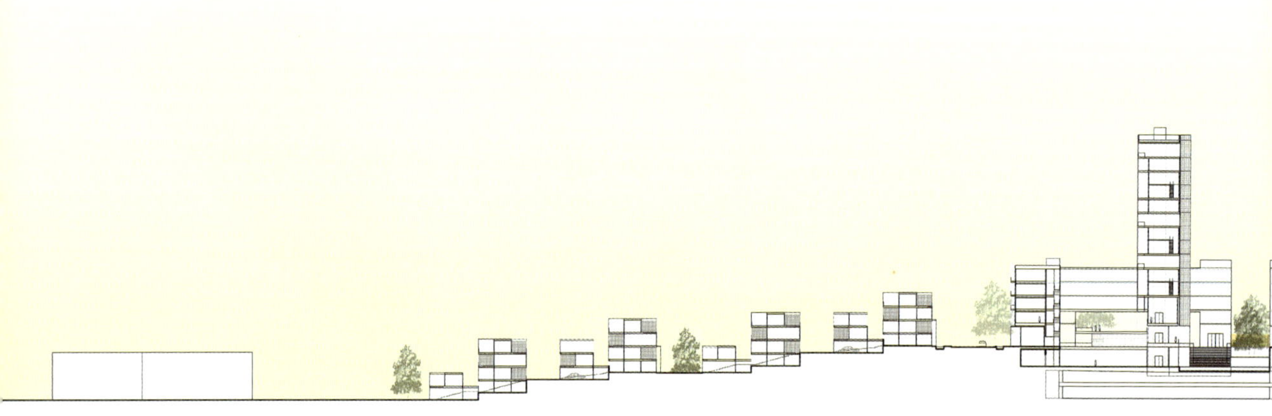

Top: The porosity of the mid-rise residential blocks enhances the varied sectional nature of the public experience throughout the site.
Bottom: A long section illustrates the transition in scale, from low- to high-rise housing. The sloped topography and varied landscape allow for long views and unobstructed movement across the site.
Acima: A porosidade dos blocos residenciais de altura média aumenta a variada natureza seccional da experiência pública em todo projeto.
Abaixo: Uma longa seção ilustra a transição em escala, de habitações de alturas baixa a alta. A topografia inclinada e a paisagem variada permitem vistas longas e movimentos sem obstrução em todo projeto.

Mid-rise buildings are lifted off the ground to create an active pedestrian landscape. Porosity between residential blocks provides physical and visual connections to the larger community beyond.

Prédios que são como torres de altura média acima do solo criam um plano de solo ativo e uma paisagem de pedestres. A porosidade entre os blocos residenciais fornece conexões físicas e visuais para a grande comunidade abaixo.

This view is oriented toward the south, down a street that connects the entire development together; the arts precinct is on the left, with mid-rise and low-rise residences on the right.
Opposite: Site model
Esta vista e orientada para o sul, numa rua que conecta o loteamento inteiro; a academia de artes está ao lado esquerdo, com residências de alturas baixa e média na direita.
Oposto: Modelo do Projeto

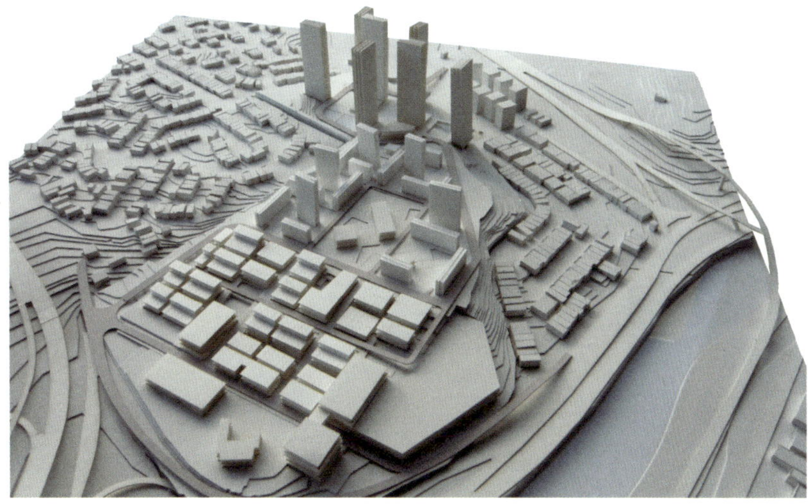

JARDIM BRASILEIRO Lis Cena

The development is divided into three sections: two residential and one commercial. The residential towers are grouped together to create two distinct communities at the middle and upper portions of the site. A colorful, multi-layer landscape of small pools, native plants, and athletic courts provide active connections between the high-rise towers and shared amenities. Traditional garden elements create hard and soft surfaces that weave together to designate public and private areas. At the lowest portion of the site, a large retail complex extends toward the city and is positioned to become a destination shopping center.

In response to the cultural and environmental context of São Paulo's beautiful urban landscapes and Modern architectural heritage, Jardim Brasileiro addresses three types of programs: socio-urban, ecological, environmental-technological. Each programmatic aspect of the architectural project manifests in a distinct spatial strategy that elaborates on the powerful and expressive language of Brazil's Modernist architecture.

The first strategy deals with the difficult issue of personal security, which poses a wide spectrum of social and architectural problems for the urban culture of Brazil. Instead of delineating explicit spatial boundaries with high fences or gates, the project is concerned with the notion of making a place—an environment of distinct visual and spatial experiences and a series of layered programmatic thresholds. The second strategy focuses on the use of wind flow for natural ventilation. This attempt to aid the cooling and aeration of the outdoor and indoor living spaces is integral to the design of the site plan and the towers; each building's configuration responds to the prevailing winds. Finally, the architectural strategy of the façade responds to the critical problem of sun exposure during the long periods of extreme heat in São Paulo: A clear but complex construct of layered screens and modular shading panels framed by varying zones of structural thickness are used to visually animate the pedestrian experience in the gardens below the towers. The deep articulation of the east and west façades creates a vertical texturing that is responsive to the climate and complements the planar landscape below.

This concept sketch investigates the sectional shifts in building, landscape, and natural topography. The layering of courtyards, water features, and garden terraces form a series of thresholds that provide a subtle transition from public to private spaces.

Este conceito de esboço investiga os deslocamentos secionais na construção, paisagem e topografia natural. As camadas dos pátios, as características de água, e os terraços formam uma série de limites que proporcionam uma transição sutil do público aos espaços privados.

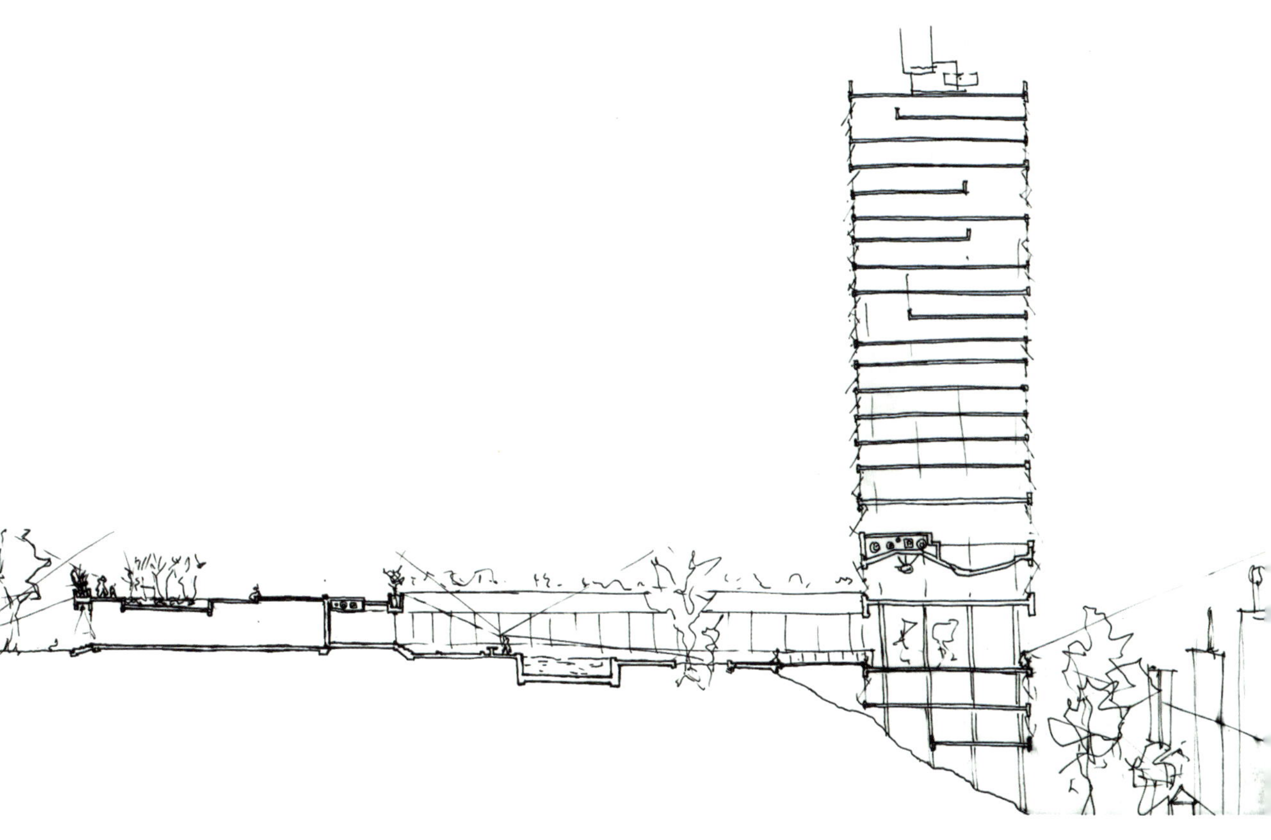

N

The prevailing wind was the decisive factor in the organization of the master plan and design of the residential towers. Each tower is split in two and shifts in plan and section to promote natural ventilation. As the prevailing wind moves across the site, it accelerates and wraps around the split towers to create a negative pressure. Internal screening elements and tectonic shifts allow the towers to "breathe" while preserving visual and acoustic privacy between units.

Opposite: Site plan

O vento predominante foi fator decisivo na organização do plano mestre e do design das torres residenciais. Cada torre é dividida em dois e muda em plano e seção para promover uma ventilação natural. Enquanto o vento predominante se move por todo local, este acelera e envolve as torres divididas para criar uma pressão negativa. Elementos de triagem interna e mudanças tectônicas permitem as torres a "respirarem" enquanto preservam a privacidade visual e acústica entre as unidades.

Oposto: Planta do projeto

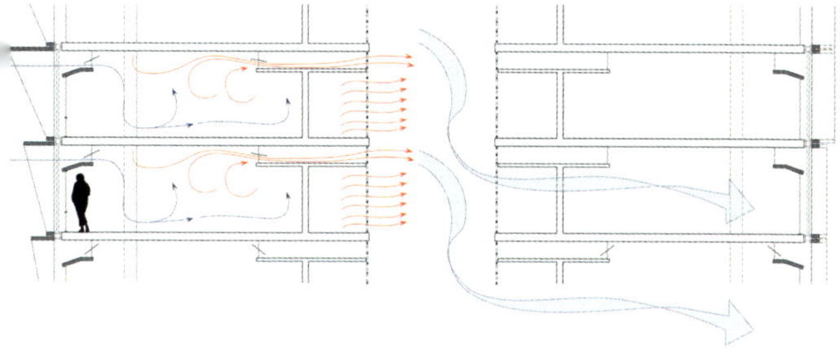

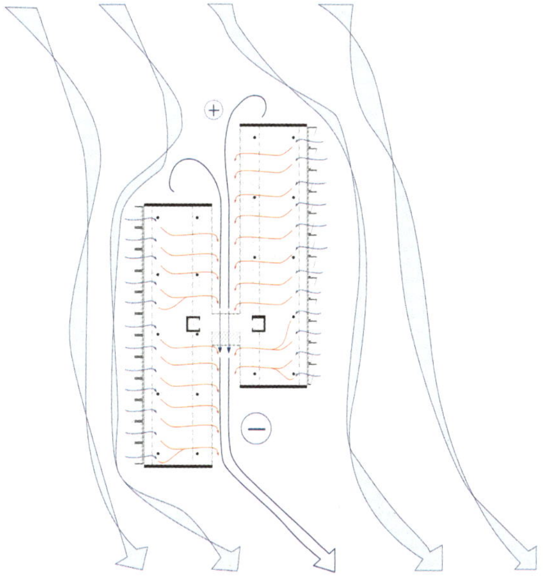

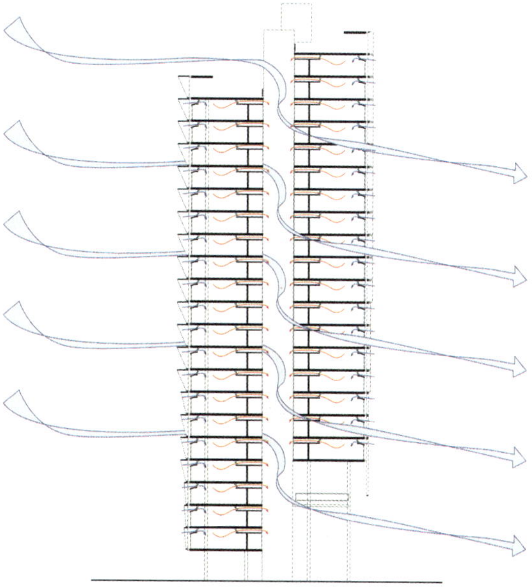

Top: Detail view of the façade solar shading system.
Bottom: Public amenities are embedded in the landscape and frame views of the residential towers above.
Opposite: View from a roof terrace toward central São Paulo.

Acima: Detalhes da vista do sistema de sombreamento solar da fachada.
Abaixo: Amenidades públicas são incorporadas na paisagem e vista enquadradas das torres residenciais acima.
Oposto: Vista do telhado geminado para o Centro de São Paulo.

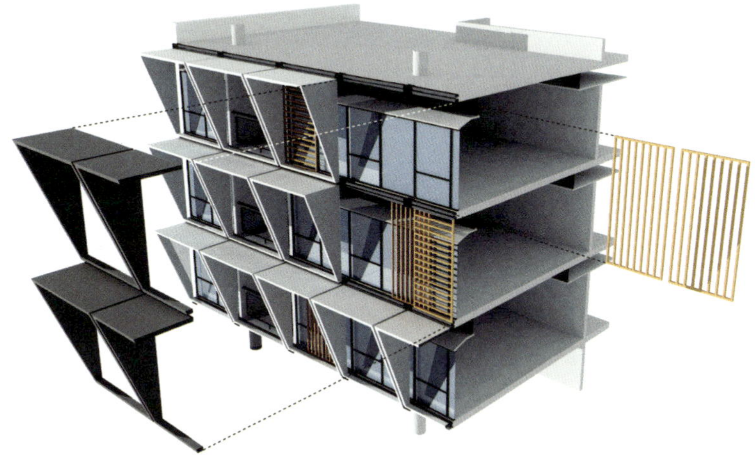

Layers of soft and hardscape overlap to provide areas of shade and light.
Opposite: Detail view of the multi-layered landscape.
Camadas de sobreposição suave e dura proporcionam áreas de sombra e luz.
Oposto: Vista detalhada da paisagem de múltiplas camadas.

Opposite: View of typical tower from the street level.
Oposto: Vista ao nível da rua de uma típica torre.

CIDADE VIZINHANÇA Catherine Anderson Poulin

The resident of Cidade Vizinhança aspires to live in a medium-density neighborhood in which low-rise housing has scale and identity and the sidewalks are filled with activity. However, this vision is a challenging goal to meet because the cost efficiencies of density and the real need for security have made a successful urban neighborhood for the middle-class market unfeasible. Cidade Vizinhança, or "City of Neighborhoods," attempts to capture the fundamental characteristics of this density while addressing scale, identity, and public space in São Paulo.

At the urban scale, the master plan organizes retail program around an urban street and public spaces, including a pedestrian walkway. In order to accomplish this, the developer partners with a specialized retail developer to create a rich public streetscape, rather than an enclosed shopping mall. The public spaces of the major street and pedestrian pathways are separated from the private residential zone by a sectional shift, ensuring privacy and security without resorting to the existing hard barriers that keep residents safe but isolated throughout São Paulo.

At the community scale, the site is divided into multiple zones to vary scale, density, and marketability. In order to meet minimum investor returns, the development must allow for 2,380 dwelling units. Using the proposed tower configuration, this goal translates to seventeen towers on the 180,000-square-meter site. Rather than evenly distributing the towers, the master plan groups three to five towers into dense and unique clusters that allow for greater expanses of open space. Built space and landscape alternate in eight striations across the site, varying in scale and character to provide identity and differentiation, a natural phasing proposal.

At the building scale, each tower within Cidade Vizinhança is conceptually divided from one twenty-eight-story building into seven mid-rise four-story buildings stacked atop one another. This design is accomplished by carving out public space in four-story increments along the height of the tower to provide small-scale public amenities. The twenty residential units can access each amenity—for example, parks, gardens, recreational facilities, and indoor gathering spaces—exclusively, providing a sense of small-scale community within the tower and alleviating density.

Vertical programming of public space and amenities is more than a programmatic element; it activates the façade and defines the image of the building—and, by extension, the development—to operate as a marketing tool for the unique scale and spatial structure of Cidade Vizinhança. At the urban, community, and building scales, the sense of identity and place becomes increasingly granular as the occupant moves from a development of 8,500 people to a cluster of 1,960 to a building of 490 and finally to a community of seventy.

Vertical amenities foster a sense of community within the residential towers and provide visual connection to the city beyond.
Opposite: Catalogue of typical amenity types diagrammed in section.
Amenidades verticais promovem um senso de comunidade dentro das torres residenciais e fornecem uma conexão visual abaixo da cidade.
Oposto: Catálogo de típicos tipos de amenidades diagramados em seções.

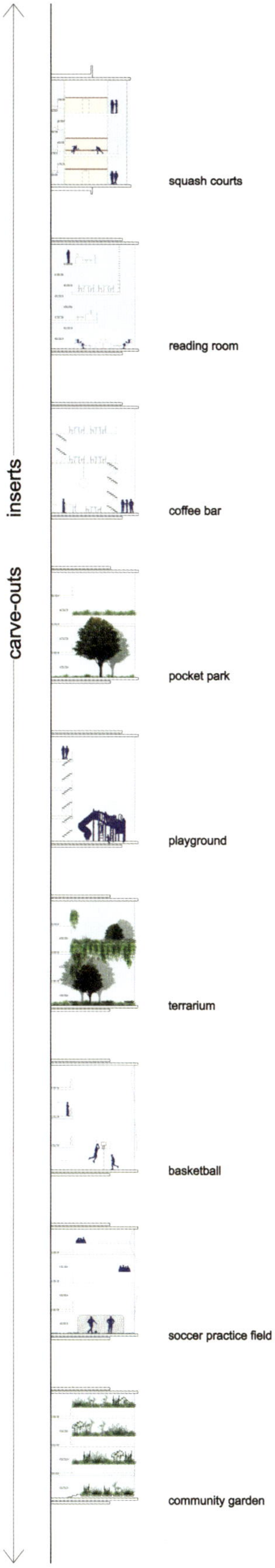

inserts
carve-outs

squash courts
reading room
coffee bar
pocket park
playground
terrarium
basketball
soccer practice field
community garden

Residential units lock together around multi-level public amenity spaces.
Opposite: The publicly accessible retail street is adjacent to and sectionally interconnected with the residential development for visual connections but without actual physical access.
Unidades residenciais são trancadas ao redor de espaços de utilidade pública com multi-níveis.
Oposto: A rua comercial de acesso público é adjacente e seccionalmente interligada ao loteamento residencial para conexões visuais mas sem acesso físico.

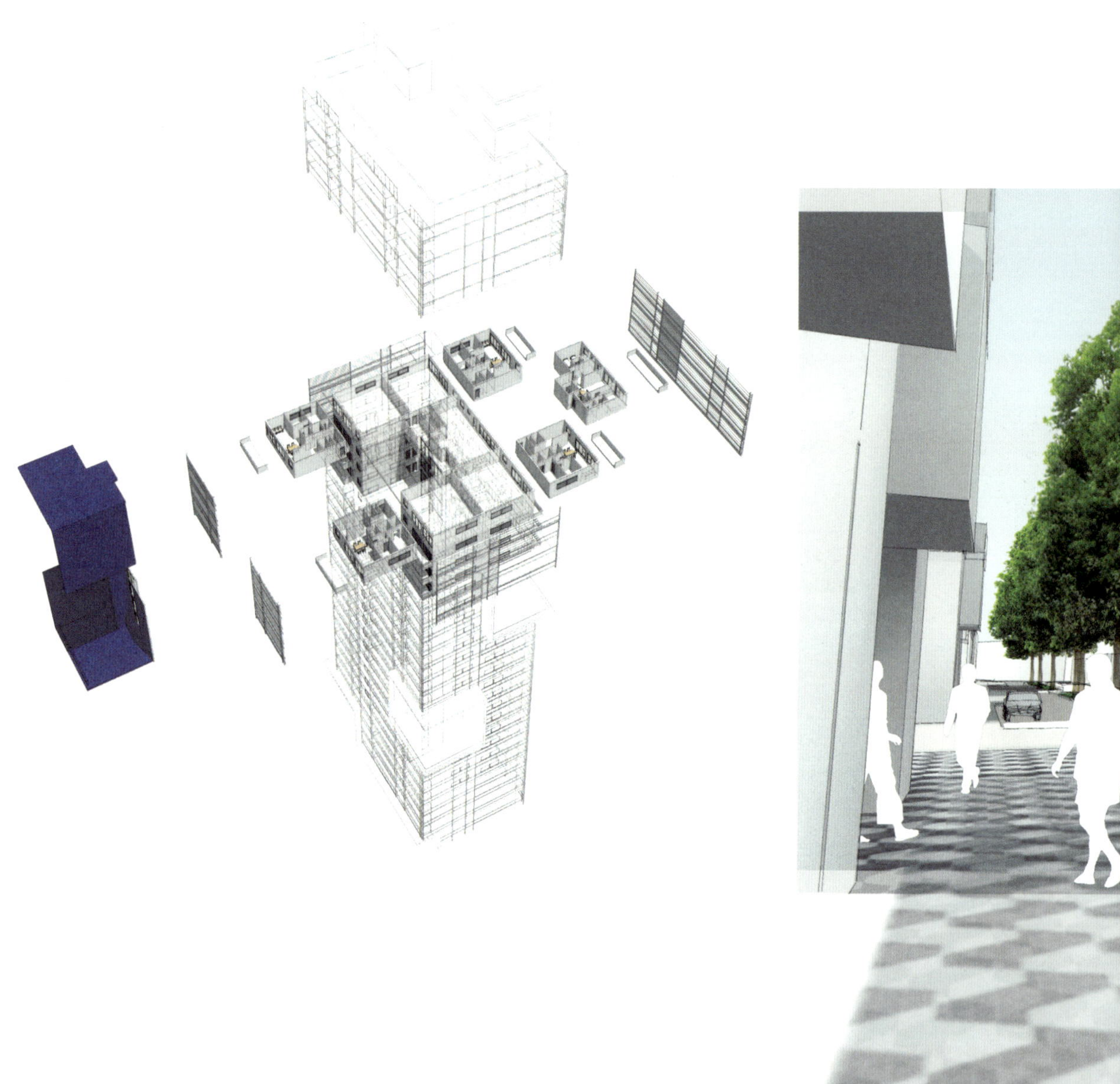

Opposite: Site plan
Oposto: Planta do Local

JARDIM VIVENTE Hilary Zaic

This project takes advantage of the lush nature of the existing site by creating a new semi-public park surrounded by an undulating series of terraced houses and residential towers. Connected formally and physically to a park to the north of the site as well as to the new retail complex to the south, the new park would initially be accessible only to residents of Jardim Vivente but everything would be open to the larger public.

Building and topography work together to provide controlled points of entry and a sense of enclosure that eliminates the need for physical compound walls and entrance gates. Along the length of the site, the park program transitions into recreation fields, water features, and a dense, existing tree grove. Vehicular circulation remains external to the park, establishing entry nodes where residents can enter underground parking stacked efficiently below the programed landscape. Within these nodes, public amenities extend into the central landscape to shape pockets of shared space with varying degrees of privacy in plan and in section.

Low-rise and high-rise residential typologies coexist to offer a variety of types of living. The terraced housing stacks on top of parking and amenity spaces while bringing the park into the building itself to maximize outdoor private space. A semi-private walkway connects the park with the low-rise units, high-rise lobby, amenity spaces, and public program. The phases of construction play an important part in the evolution of the park. Starting at the rear of the site and moving forward, each phase is paired with an underground parking structure and its required infrastructure. The park becomes the signature of the entire project, blurring the boundaries of the site with the neighboring landscape and allowing even the towers to echo the local fauna through the design of the towers' sun shading.

Left: The public realm folds into and over the semi-public park at each entry node.
Right: The complex contains 1,804 residential units, ranging from 95 meters to 125 square meters. There are 1,656 units in the high-rise towers, and 223 are in the low-rise buildings.
Opposite: In this view from the central park, the façades of the low-rise residential towers are articulated with ribbons of concrete panels. The vertical striations vary in texture from bottom to top and form a pattern that is reminiscent of the nearby Brazilian forests.

Esquerda: O domínio público dobra dentro e sobre os parques semi-público em cada nó de entrada.
Direita: O complexo contém 1.804 unidades residenciais, que vão de 95 metros a 125 metros quadrados. Há 1.656 unidades nas torres de arranha-céu, e 223 nós edifícios de altura baixa.
Oposto: Nesta visão do parque central, as fachadas das torres residenciais de baixa altura são articulados com painéis de fitas de concreto. As estrias verticais variam em textura de baixo para cima e formam um molde que lembra as florestas Brasileiras próximas.

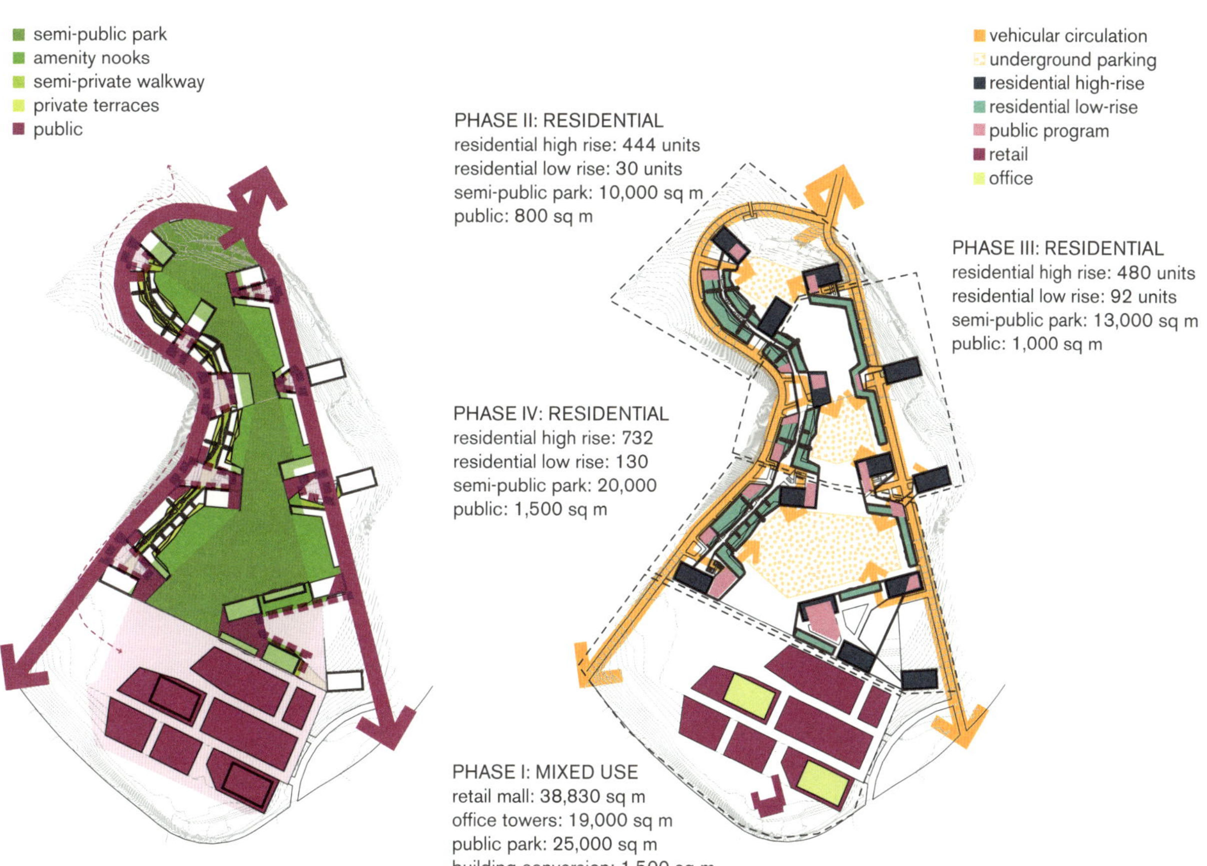

This view looks down into the semi-private pathway, interspersed with palm trees that rise up from the level below. Opposite: This aerial view of a detailed model shows the elevated semi-public walkway connecting to the units and the park.

Esta vista olha para dentro de um caminho semi-privado, intercalado com palmeiras que se elevam de um nível abaixo.

Oposto: Esta vista aérea de um modelo detalhado mostra a elevada passagem semi-pública conectada às unidades e ao parque.

The entrance nodes act as the interface between the public and private zones.

Os nódulos de entrada agem como uma interface entre as zonas pública e privada.

GROUND COVER: SÃO PAULO Anja Turowski

Challenging the notion of traditional tower-in-the-park developments, this project seeks to engage the ground plane in a way that reappropriates the generally unclaimed and often neglected space between high-rise buildings. To activate this space, this scheme anchors streamlined residential towers to the site by complementary high-density terraced housing. The aggregation of mid-rise housing units results in a park landscape that descends through the middle of the site, following the natural topography. A winding access road weaves through the site and connects the park and terraced houses.

The terraced housing units offer private outdoor green spaces for each unit, while the orientation and slope to the interior of the site provides a varied, granulated edge to the new park landscape. The units are standardized, but by following the natural slope of the site, the fluid, composite housing form offers views of the landscape. Unlike traditional terrace typologies that use existing topography to cluster medium-density housing, this strategy layers housing units above the existing ground plane to create an artificial underbelly between the residential structure and ground. The underside of the terraced, single-family units harbors communal amenity spaces, such as child care, shops, and recreation facilities, while providing parking for residents of both the towers and the terrace buildings.

In contrast to the granular edge and slope on the interior of the site, the street façades of the housing hug tightly to the road to create a dense and urban environment. The façades are articulated in such a way as to provide windows to the interior of the structure, thus distinguishing larger-scale communal program elements, such as performance spaces, from smaller ones, such as the shops. This strategy allows for public and private programs to have opposite orientation, affording privacy to the housing units while offering public access to the communal amenities.

The various building components of this development are assembled and integrated within several composite structures that can be phased in four stages. The buildings themselves are composed of large-span concrete construction, which is structured according to the parking requirements below and adjusted to the small-scale standardized units above. All residential units can be accessed directly from the parking areas via hallways that are top-lit by penetrations in the terraced housing layer as well as from common front-door entrances that are located at the street façades.

The terraced housing responds to the natural topography of the site.
A habitação geminada responde à topografia natural do projeto.

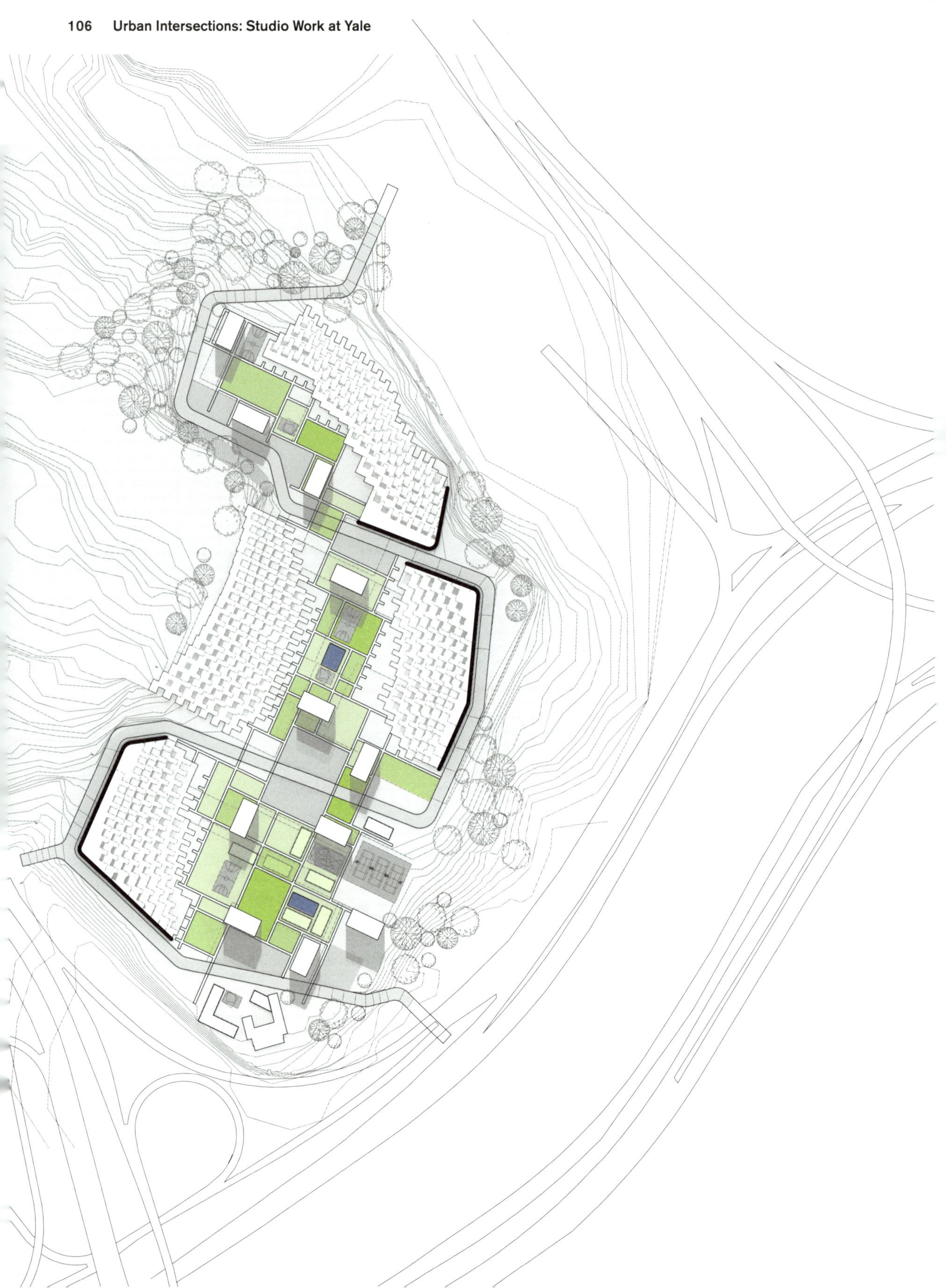

Top: Detail plan of terraced housing.
Bottom: View of typical terraced housing units.
Opposite: Site plan
Acima: Planta detalhada da habitação geminada.
Abaixo: Vista de unidades típicas de habitações geminadas.
Oposto: Plano do projeto

The terrace housing follows and responds to the topography of the existing site.
Opposite: This model shows the building program and its corresponding construction sequence: underground parking, community programs, and individual terraced housing units face the interior park and tower landscape.

As habitações geminadas seguem e respondem à topografia do local existente.
Oposto: Este diagrama mostra o programa de construção e a sequência de construção correspondente: estacionamento subterrâneo, programas comunitários, e unidades de habitações geminadas individuais ficam de frente ao interior do parque e paisagem de torres.

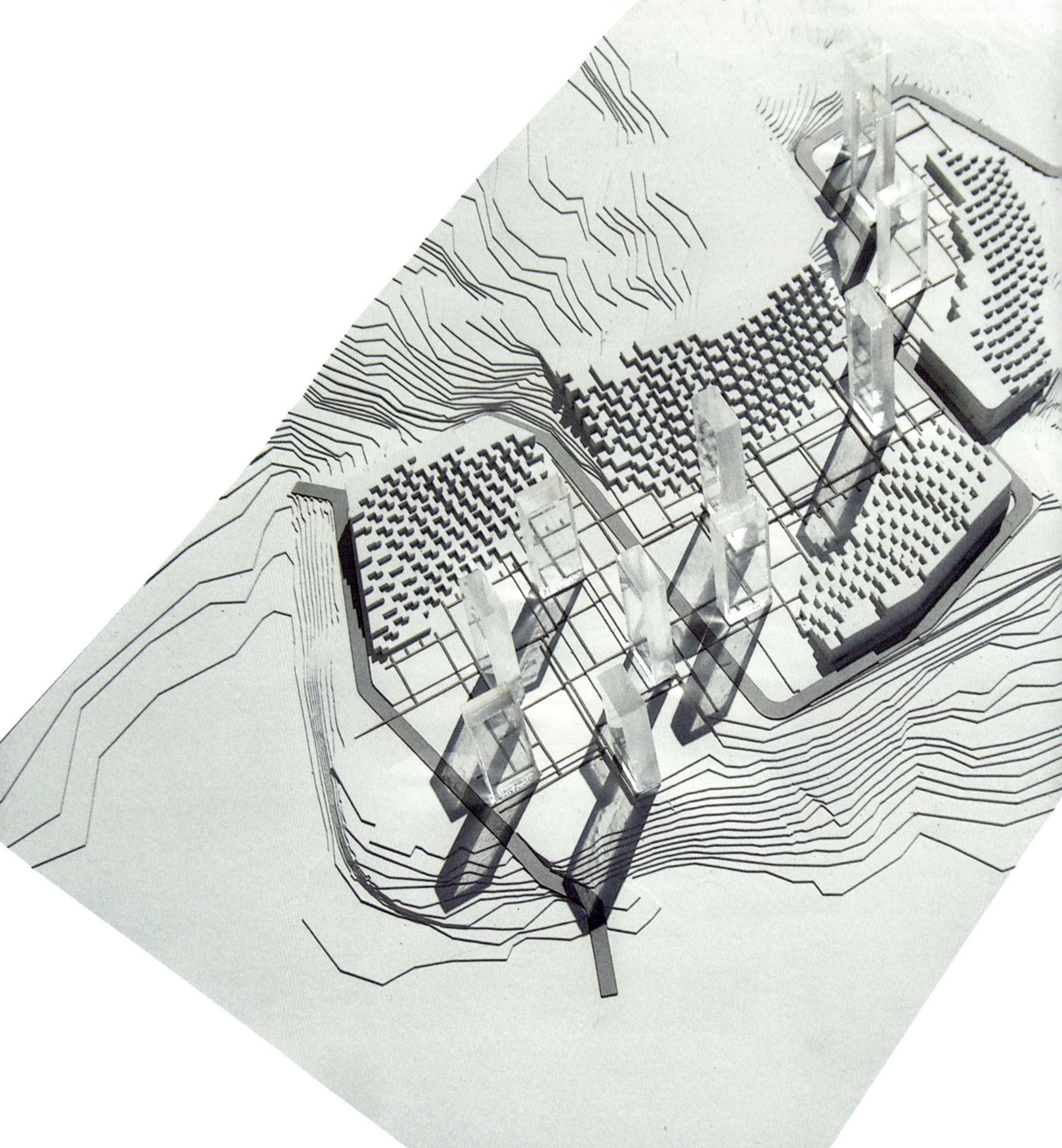

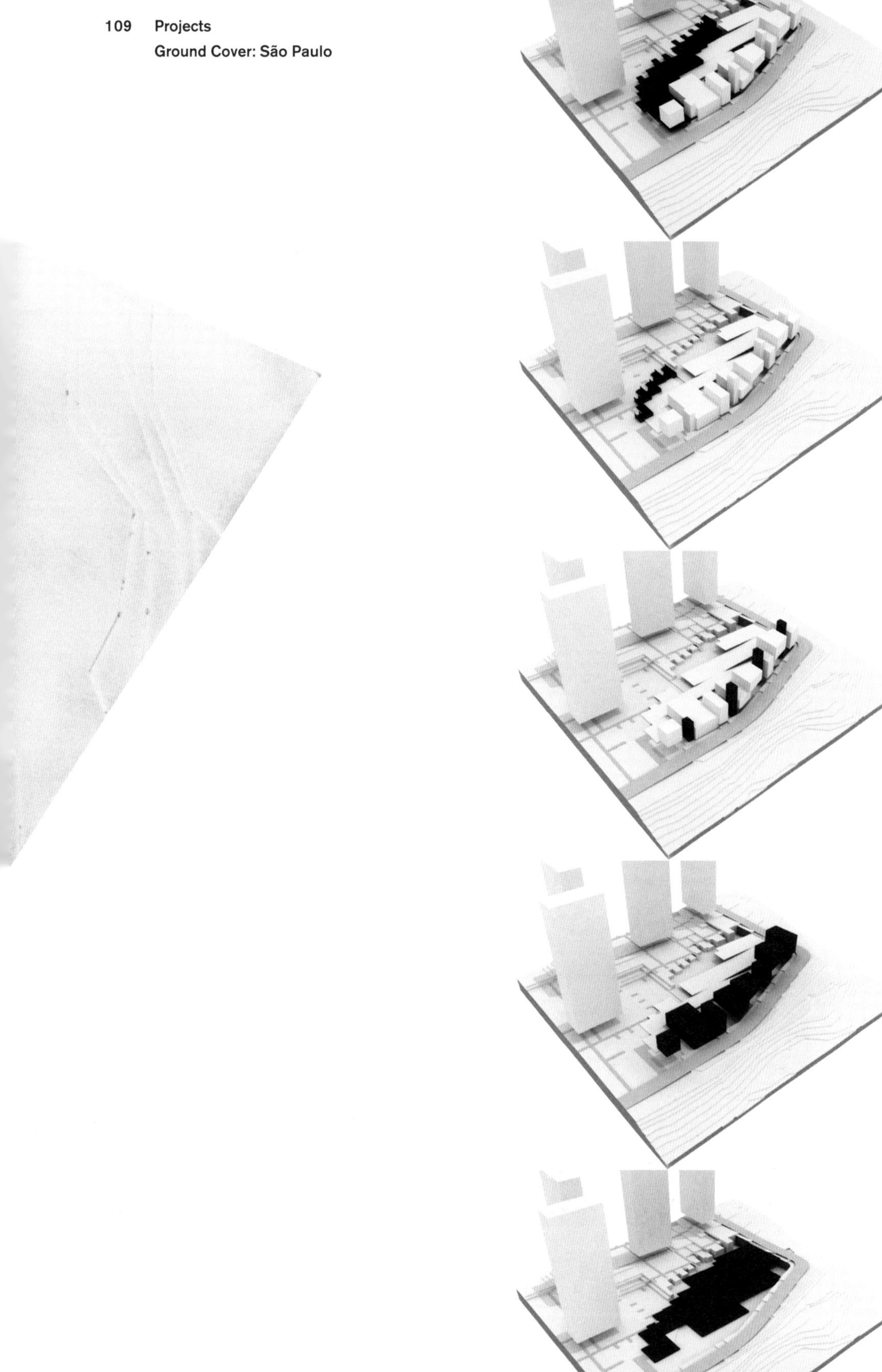

This site section looks south toward São Paulo.
Esta seção do projeto olha sul em direção a São Paulo.

Opposite top: An elevated pedestrian walkway connects Barrio Real with the residential neighborhood to the east. Opposite bottom: Planting and paving patterns emphasize the underlying site organization and form a cohesive, walkable streetscape.

Oposto a cima: Uma passagem de pedestres elevada conecta o Barrio Real com o bairro residencial ao leste. Oposto a baixo: Plantando e pavimentando moldes o que enfatiza a organização do projeto subjacente e forma um espaço de rua caminhavel e coeso.

BARRIO REAL Steve Ybarra

The complexities of Bandeirantes, São Paulo, extend well beyond site, program, and density. More than just a residential development, Bandeirantes is a neighborhood in its infancy. "Barrio Real" suggests a first step in creating a sense of identity for a new and exponentially growing demographic, the Brazilian middle class. The development's urban form is inspired—not in scale, but in aspiration—by the Jardins neighborhood in São Paulo. There, the sprawling high-rise development of São Paulo is kept at bay, allowing for a vibrant, walkable, low-rise district to take shape at its center.

The residential component of the project comprises two areas: A cluster of six point towers is located on the northern, heavily wooded part of the site, and a row of six slab towers straddle a plateau edge on the southern portion of the site, dividing the residential section of the site from the retail development below. Between these two densely populated tower clusters are a series of low-rise townhouses, creating a fabric of pleasant, walkable streets that are beneficial to the neighborhood. A neighborhood Main Street, consisting of retail, educational, and public functions, links these three areas of the project and connects them back to the existing residential fabric to the west.

Alongside Main Street runs a linear public park that is mirrored on the development's eastern edge by another linear park that primarily caters to the residents of the neighborhood. Outdoor sports facilities are located here, and the open space connects to greenways at the center of each townhouse block as well as to an existing public park located on the northern edge of the site.

Barrio Real incorporates sustainable practices at a number of scales. All the residential units on the site use natural ventilation, while the large areas of green open space aid in stormwater management and flood prevention. The focused density of the tower clusters allows for efficient public-transit locations, serviced either by bus or a future metro stop. Most important, the consistent block dimensions allow for sustained growth over time; each parcel has the ability to change and grow without adversely affecting the general character of the neighborhood's public realm. In this sense, Barrio Real acts as a template for future São Paulo growth and development and provides for a sustainable, vibrant residential and urban public space that is integrated with its surroundings.

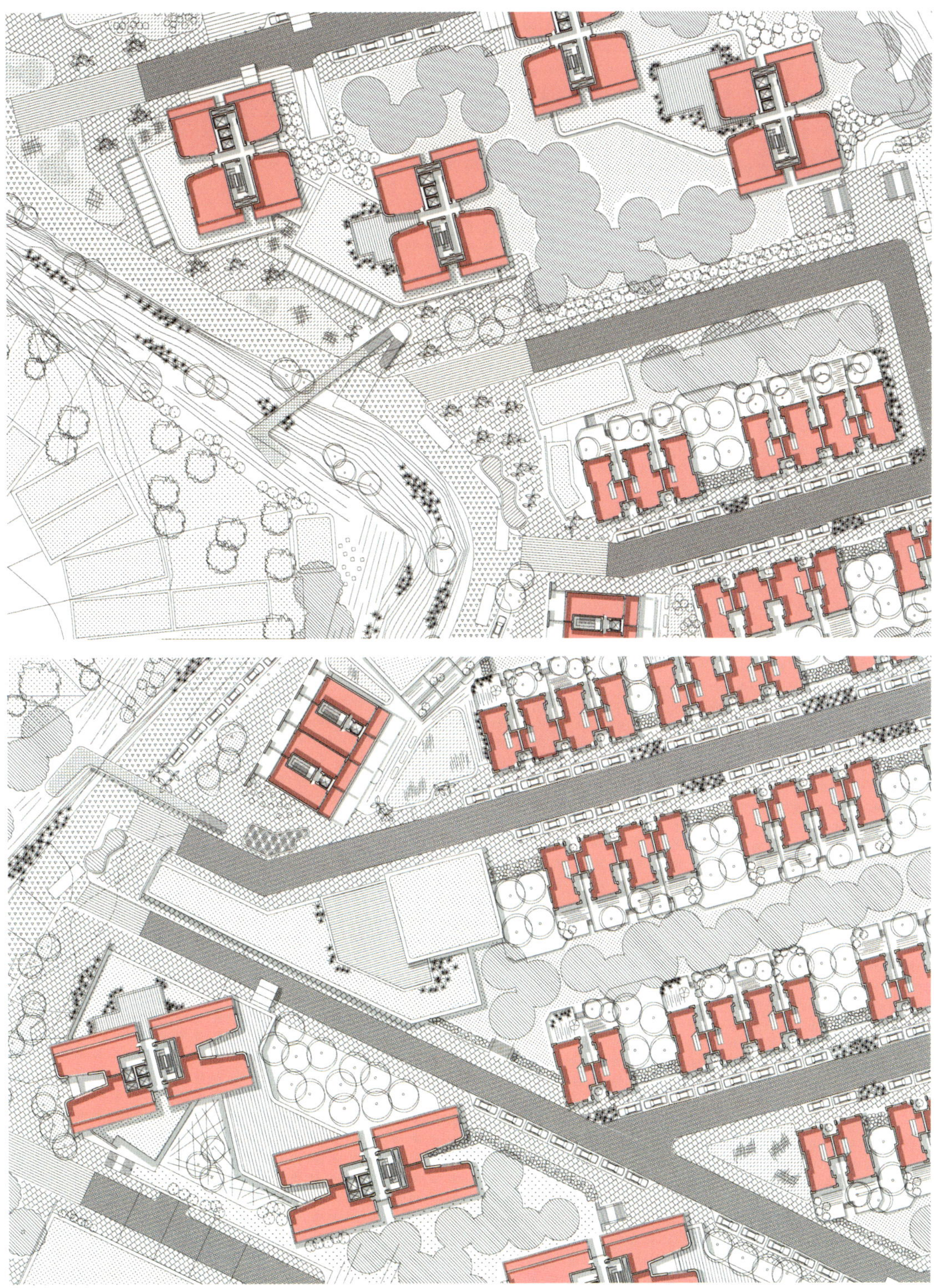

Tall point towers rise up from a low-rise garden neighborhood. A large retail complex sits on a plateau at the base of the site.
Opposite: Site Plan

Altas torres pontiagudas elevam-se do interior de um jardim de altura baixo. Um grande complexo de vendas festa em cima de um platô na base do projeto.
Oposto: Plano do Local

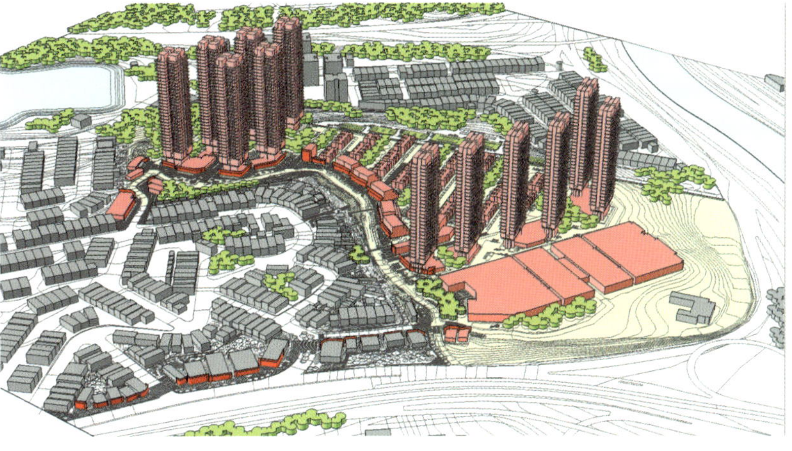

BANDEIRANTES: SEE IT FIRST Carmel Greer

The project seeks to use the site's natural topography and lush landscape to create a development characterized by significant density and close proximity to nature. A series of plinths extends into the jungle and navigates the site's terrain, allowing the lush, steep areas to remain undisturbed while taking advantage of the dramatic views toward São Paulo. The plinths themselves house reflecting pools, manicured landscape elements, and other amenities; residential parking is located below, connecting discreet and convenient parking to the circulation core of each building. The surface of each plinth is approximately a half-story above the existing grade, minimizing excavation and disruption. This strategy reduces initial site costs while providing security elements and parking that are critical to the successful development of the area's residential market.

Towers line the western edge of the site, culminating in a monumental residential tower that serves as a branding mechanism for Tishman Speyer. The larger tower of the scheme is visible from the highway, the river, and central São Paulo, distinguishing the Tishman Speyer site from other residential projects. Each unit within the lower residential towers has a customizable balcony lined with rich Brazilian wood. The wood is also used for louvers, providing shade at each window. These elements provide material richness and passive solar climate control for the tower, a building type often characterized by sterility. The balcony and outdoor cooking features are customizable by the unit's owners, providing a differentiation between units that is visible from the exterior.

A retail center occupies the lowest portion of the site. A sinuous road threads among the towers and landscape, providing the experience of a fast-paced hillside drive in an otherwise traffic-congested urban environment. A central spine of walkways and gardens connects each plinth to the retail hub and enables pedestrians to navigate through the project and into adjacent parks and residential areas.

A landmark tower creates the visual identity for the development.
Uma torre que é considerada um marco dá identidade visual ao loteamento.

Top: Each unit has a private terrace wrapped in wood, helping to break down the scale and providing a uniformity of the towers across the site.
Bottom: Perspective view of streetscape.
Opposite: The landscape plinths create horizontal datums that direct views toward São Paulo.
Acima: Cada unidade tem um terraço privado envolvido em Madeira, ajudando a quebrar a escala e fornecendo uniformidade às torres por todo projeto.
Abaixo: Vista perspectiva da rua.
Oposto: Os plintos da paisagem criam datums horizontais que direcionam a vista a São Paulo.

The undulating road creates moments in which the neighboring forest is allowed to extend into the development, blurring the boarders of the site.
Opposite: Ten residential towers are distributed across the site and organized around a central pedestrian spine.
A estrada ondulante cria momentos em que a floresta vizinha consegue estender-se para dentro do loteamento, borrando as fronteiras do local.
Oposto: Dez torres residenciais são organizadas e distribuídas por todo projeto em torno de uma faixa central para pedestres.

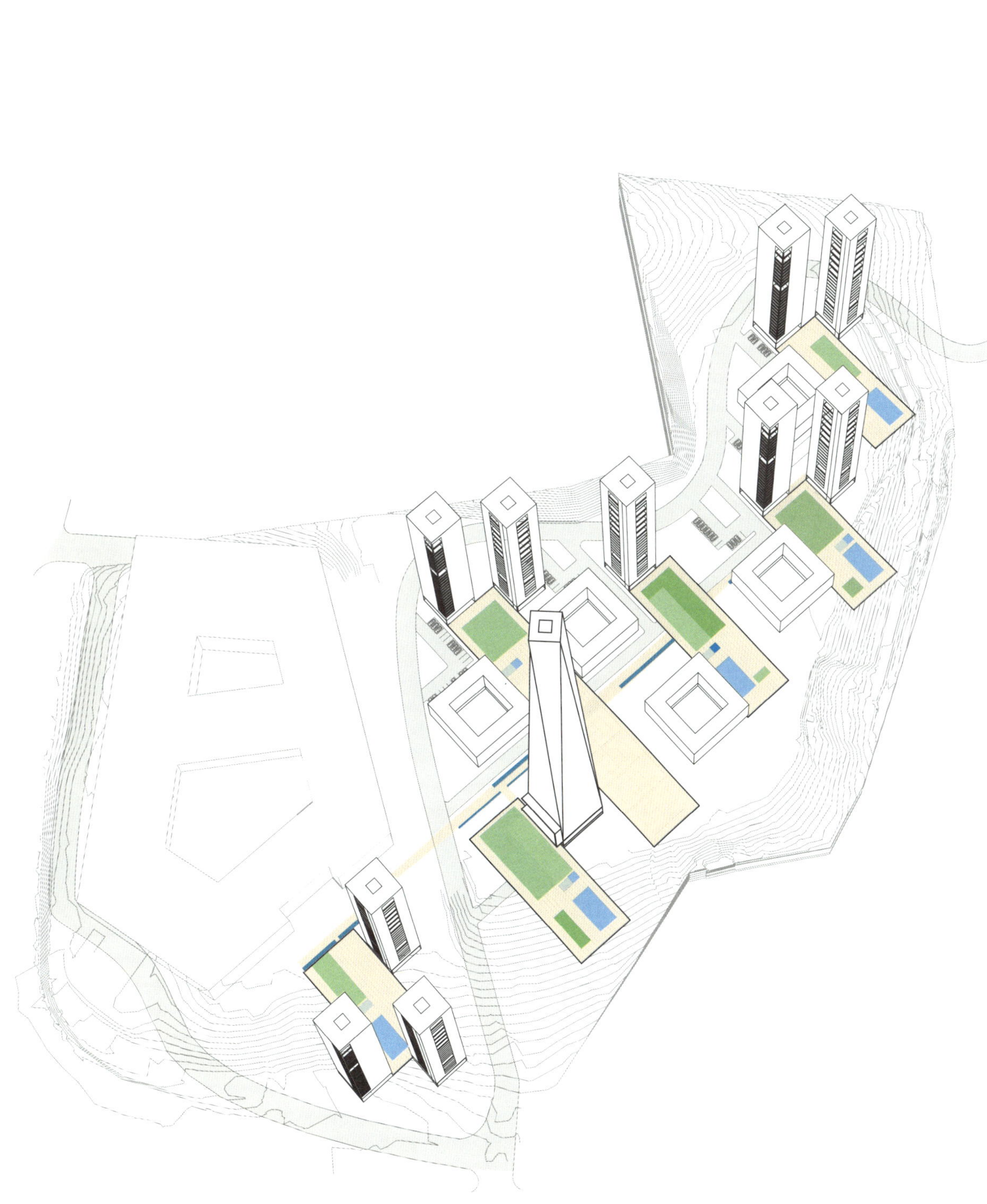

A FRAMEWORK FOR IDENTITY Alejandro Fernandez de Mesa

One of the most notable features of Brazilian design is its success in creating provocative public spaces. As part of the dialogue between the architect and developer, successful public space cannot only strengthen a sense of community but also act as a branding strategy for the development. A private residential development of 1,500 units in Brazil cannot, however, successfully exist as a collection of individual units without connective tissue, which is the defined public space. The goal of this project is to provide a framework by which a clear hierarchy of public space can be achieved. Moreover, this framework accounts for the amenities that are characteristic of such developments as well as the performance demands of the developer.

In this proposal, buildings are organized into clusters of small-scale towers as a direct critique of the Modernist arrangement of Brasília and its superblock form. In this Modernist tradition, buildings are placed on the site in a rational manner that responds to environmental concerns and provides generous public space. However, what the Modernist approach fails to give this particular site is a sense of control and the ability to maintain these public spaces in a manner that links the architecture and its inhabitants.

This project provides for three scales of public space. The first, the so-called cluster, explores the relationship between two buildings: the mid-rise and the tower. Here, a two-level landscape connects the two buildings to provide a shaded arrival to each building and visual connectivity from amenity space to the private realm within the clusters. The second scale, the block, connects the more intimate spaces of each cluster and demarcates the circulation through the site; the scale of the block also functions as an efficient way to sequence construction. Finally, the largest scale of the project is a central void, or plaza, that is connected to part of the network of clusters and medium-sized public spaces that together define the community. The overall result is a series of sensory experiences that are instigated by a recognizable scale and materiality. The project is organized formally around this scalar shift in landscape and development phasing.

This aerial site plan shows how the three scales of public space form a landscape network throughout the site starting with the retail component along the highway and ending with the cluster of towers and community retail to the north.

Esta planta aérea mostra como as três escalas de espaço público formam a network da paisagem em todo projeto começando pelo componente comercial ao longo da auto-estrada e terminando com o agrupamento de torres e área comercial da comunidade ao norte.

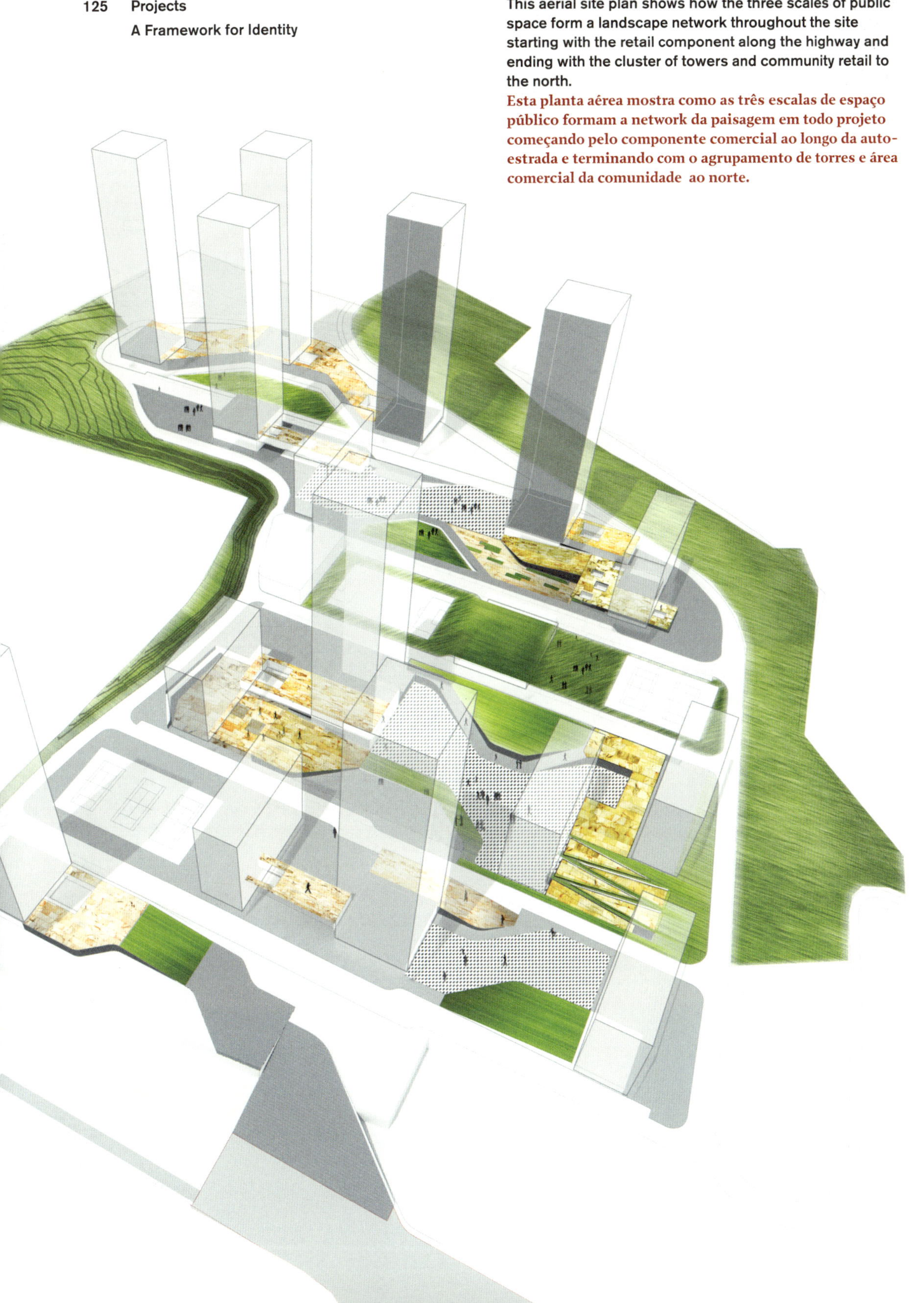

The Block: Larger public spaces exist between clusters and become the connective framework for the entire community.

O Bloco: Grandes espaços públicos existentes entre grupos que tornam-se um modelo conjuntivo para toda a comunidade.

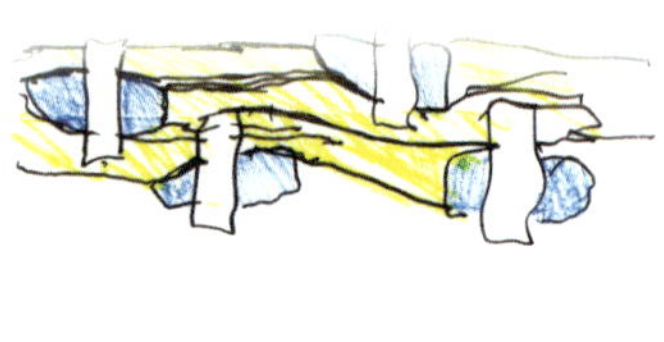

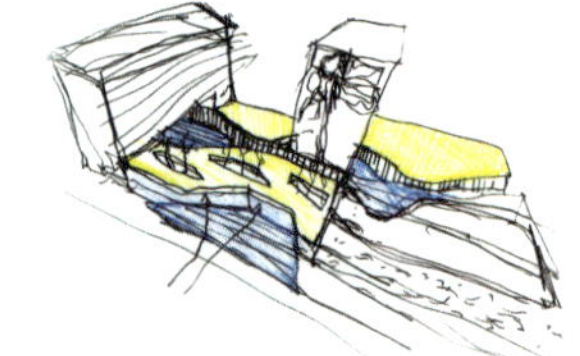

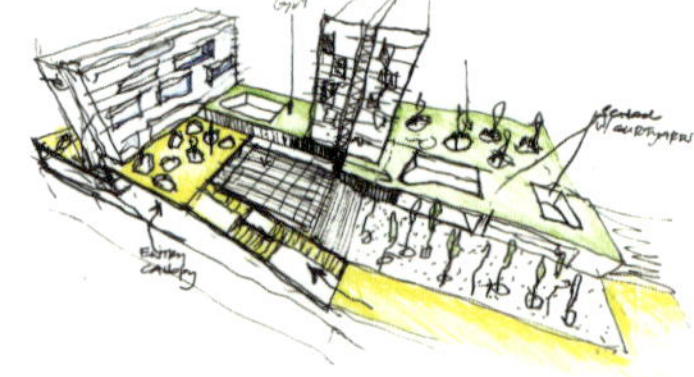

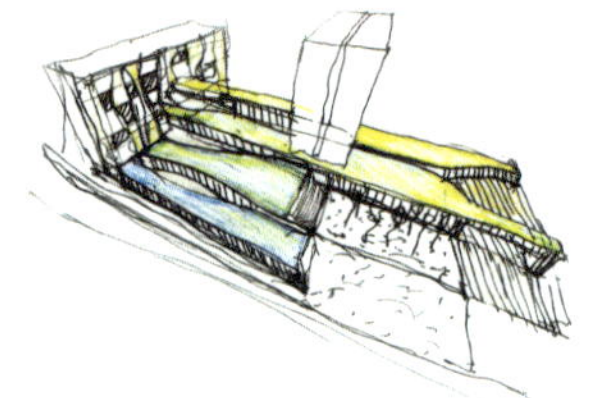

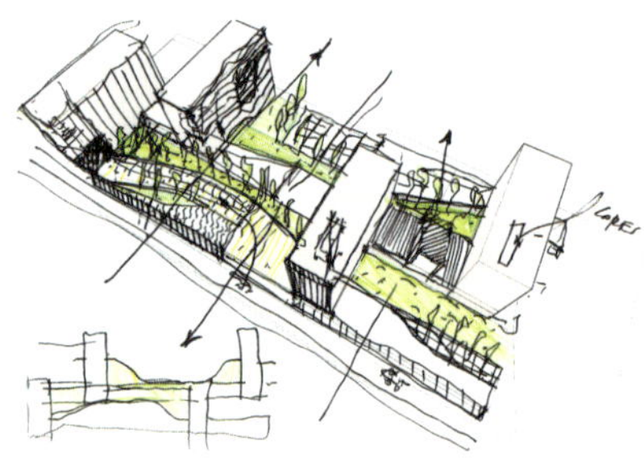

The Community: The largest scale of public space that forms the center of the community is a place of release and identity within the heterogeneous network of clusters. Opposite: Concept sketches

A Comunidade: A maior escala de espaço público que forma o centro da comunidade é um local de lançamento e identidade dentro da rede heterogênea dos grupos. Oposto: Conceito de esboço

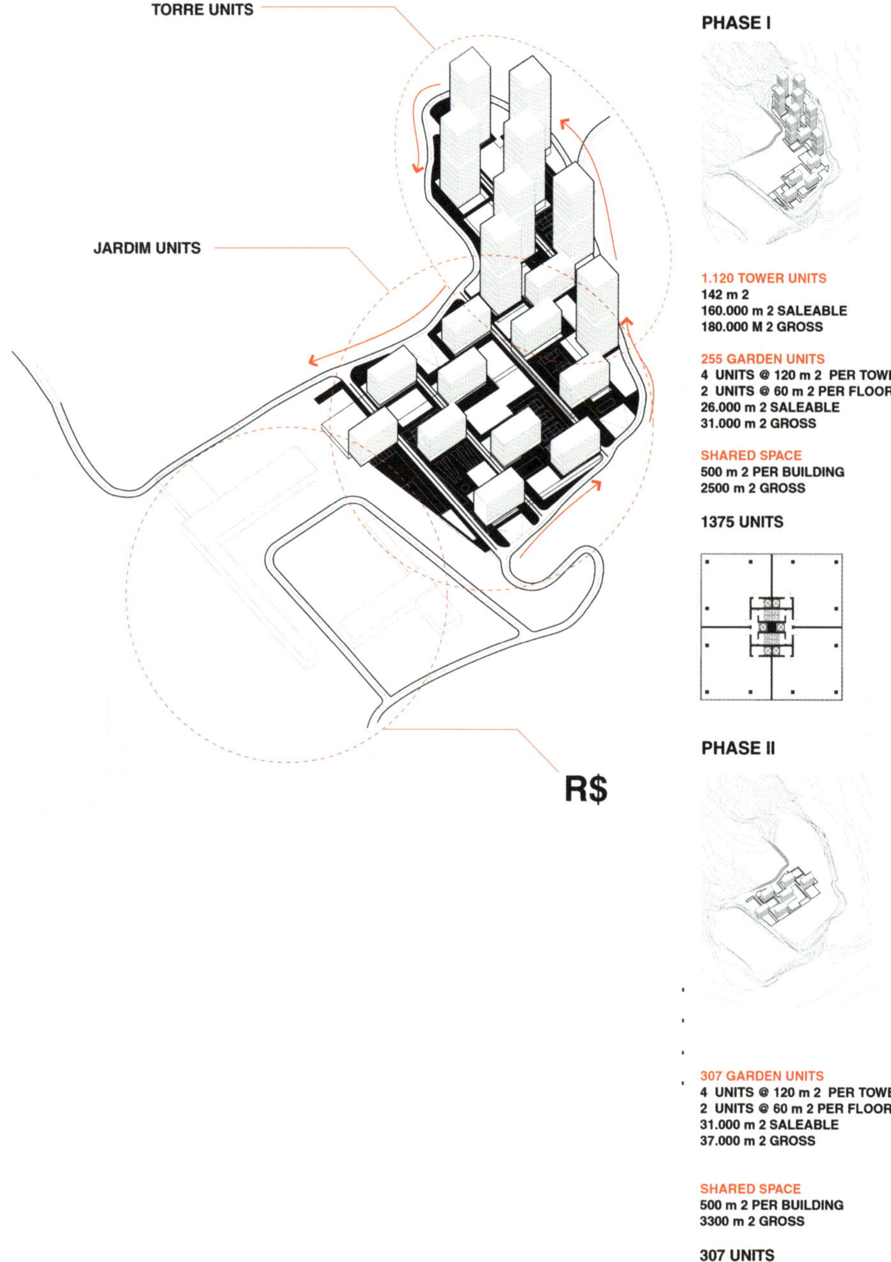

PHASE I

1.120 TOWER UNITS
142 m 2
160.000 m 2 SALEABLE
180.000 M 2 GROSS

255 GARDEN UNITS
4 UNITS @ 120 m 2 PER TOWER
2 UNITS @ 60 m 2 PER FLOOR
26.000 m 2 SALEABLE
31.000 m 2 GROSS

SHARED SPACE
500 m 2 PER BUILDING
2500 m 2 GROSS

1375 UNITS

PHASE II

307 GARDEN UNITS
4 UNITS @ 120 m 2 PER TOWER
2 UNITS @ 60 m 2 PER FLOOR
31.000 m 2 SALEABLE
37.000 m 2 GROSS

SHARED SPACE
500 m 2 PER BUILDING
3300 m 2 GROSS

307 UNITS

220.000 m 2 SALEABLE AREA
260.000 m2 GROSS AREA

1.682 UNITS

DEVELOPMENT PHASING STRATEGY

The Cluster: The first scale of public space is characterized by a two-level landscape that inextricably links amenities above with the shaded public spaces below.
Opposite: Phasing and development strategy plan

O Grupo: A primeira escala de espaço público é caracterizada por uma paisagem de dois níveis que inextricavelmente conecta as amenidades acima com os espaços públicos sombreados.
Oposto: Desenvolvimento do plano de estratégia e fase.

Opposite: Site Plan
Oposto: Planta do Local

A PRAÇA EM BANDEIRANTES Bradley Baer

A Praça em Bandeirantes redefines high-density housing for one of the fastest-growing populations in the world while at the same time addressing issues of security, public space, and sense of community. To accomplish this, the master plan proposes a series of mid-level residential buildings that splay out from a central piazza, the focal point of the development. This main piazza contains a full-sized soccer field, community center, and retail space. The strategic configuration of residential units and public space provides a sense of security and community while avoiding the need for a traditional compound wall. Whereas towers create passages for wind and cast long shadows, a series of smaller mid-level buildings make reference to Brazil's rich history of mid-rise housing and allow for the penetration of sunlight into the units and public spaces.

The residential program requirement is met and exceeded by ten, ten- to twelve-story buildings that have the capacity for more than 2,800 units and maintain an intimate scale in comparison to the typical high-rise tower. The resultant spaces between and around the housing form a series of themed neighborhoods that provide variety in amenities, lifestyle, and scale. A meandering drive mediates the sloped topography of the site and provides each apartment block with a porte-cochere. The splayed configuration of the residential layouts provides multiple orientations for the apartments: some units face the city, others have views to the new piazza and fields, and some look out onto the nearby park.

A series of voids break down the massing of the horizontal structures. Sun can penetrate through the units and to the private balconies. These cuts cause variations in the floor plates, adding value by differentiating the layout of apartments. In the morning, low light fills the piazza; at mid afternoon, sculptural trellises provide shade from the tropical sun.

Taking inspiration from the offset triangle-square-triangle pavers lining the streets of São Paulo, each building façade is composed of modular panels that are scaled-up versions of the paving patterns. As a customizable modular system, the solid panels can be replaced with slanted louvers or glazing to adjust for different environmental conditions or personal preferences.

Section through typical residential building and central retail/gathering space.
Seção através de uma típica construção residencial e de comércio central/coletando espaço.

TOP OF ROOF
(+) 135'-0"
FLOOR TEN
(+) 125'-0"
FLOOR NINE
(+) 115'-0"
FLOOR EIGHT
(+) 105'-0"
FLOOR SEVEN
(+) 95-0"
FLOOR SIX
(+) 85'-0"
FLOOR FIVE
(+) 75'-0"
FLOOR FOUR
(+) 65-0"
FLOOR THREE
(+) 55'-0"
FLOOR TWO
(+) 45'-0"
FLOOR ONE
(+) 35'-0"
SECOND MEZZANINE
(+) 25'-0"
FIRST MEZZANINE
(+) 15'-0"
GROUND LEVEL
(+) 0'-0"
LOWER LEVEL
(-) 15'-0"

Top: Rendering of terraced balconies with framed view toward the central sports fields.
Bottom: Night rendering.
Acima: Representação de varandas com terraços com vista ampla para os campos desportivos centrais.
Abaixo: Renderização da noite.

Top: Exploded diagram of the modular façade. Customizable panels can be interchanged based on environmental needs and the owners' preference to create a unique configuration for each unit.
Bottom: 3-D print study of façade concept.
Opposite: Photograph of physical model. Sports and cultural programs are carved into the landscape. Hardscaped walkways peel off the ground to provide covered zones of retail.
Acima: Painéis customizados podem ser intercambiados com base nas necessidades ambientais e a preferência do proprietário em criar uma configuração única para cada unidade.
Abaixo: Estudo de impressão 3D do conceito da fachada.
Oposto: Fotografia do modelo físico. Programas culturais e esportivos da fachada modular.

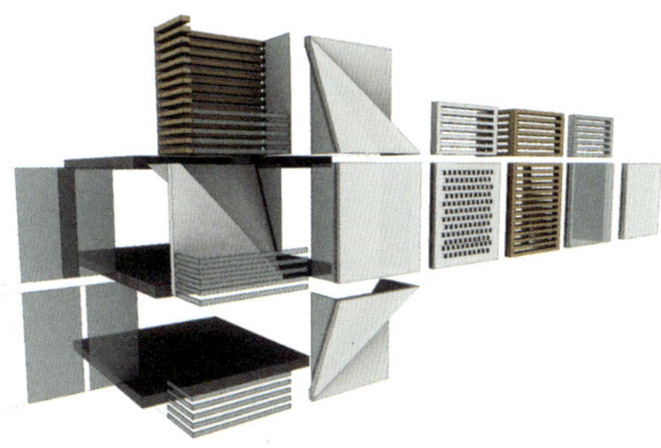

Rendering of residential tower and potential farmers' market space.

Representação de torre residencial e potencial espaço para mercado horticultor.

Opposite top: Residential units cantilever off large structural walls, enabling the public programs on the lower levels to take on an architectural language of their own.
Opposite bottom: Public amenities and resources are distributed throughout the site to promote community engagement among the towers.
Oposto acima: Unidades residenciais são distribuidas em grandes paredes estruturais, permitindo programas públicos nos níveis inferiores a assumirem uma linguagem arquitetônica própria.
Oposto abaixo: Amenidades públicas e recursos são distribuídos em todo local para promover o engajamento da comunidade entre as torres

MIRANTE Eliza Higgins

Mirante is a proposal for a 1,800-unit development that strives to meet the developers' pro forma while at the same time addressing perceptions of security and community and anticipating seasonal flooding through an architecture that is both contemporary and Brazilian.

In Portuguese, *mirante* translates to "belvedere" or "city view." Fourteen residential towers direct and define a sculpted landscape, creating a series of programmed courtyards that flow into one another. Each cluster of towers is designed to house a small community while maintaining a strong connection to the development as a whole through shared green spaces, social amenities, and visual connections.

During the rainy season in São Paulo—December through March—the two-level landscape collects and channels water to retaining ponds that double as athletic fields during the dry season. This weather shift between wet and dry and the mix of public and private amenities offer an active landscape and social community that can be experienced at the ground level as well as viewed from above.

Each tower maintains a strong connection to the ground through infrastructural concrete walls, which vary in thickness to provide vertical circulation and structural support for the residential units that cantilever above. The butterfly-shaped towers are strategically arranged to capture prevailing winds for natural ventilation and maximize views to the courtyards below and the city beyond. To account for the intense Brazilian sun, thin wooden louvers made from local, rapidly renewable pinus timber wrap between each unit's balcony and enclosure to create an active and fluid façade. Colored fabric panels on interior tracks provide additional shading and animate each façade with gradients of color from tower to tower. This blend of warm color and natural materials helps to soften the towers and break down the perception of density across the site.

A main arterial road controls vehicular circulation by releasing smaller connectors to provide access to each tower. Apart from the main circulation, each tower has a dedicated entrance and parking deck, which is concealed underground to preserve the pedestrian landscape above. Facilities with pubic access—such as a gym, schools, and local retail—infill the layers between the public park, community courtyards, and existing topography. At the base of the site, a retail and sports complex opens to the highway and city beyond but is hidden from the residences above by a large landscaped plateau that acts as a terminus to the meandering park that covers the site.

In this proposal, the layered ground and residential towers play an equal role in defining the community. Together, design and environment enhance the marketability of the development as a responsive and unique living experience in São Paulo.

Butterfly-shaped towers act as infrastructural walls to direct and form the landscape.
Torres em formato de borboleta agem como paredes de infraestrutura para direcionar e formar a paisagem.

Layers of landscape peel apart to house public programs. The ground plane becomes active with athletic courts, lounging areas, and wandering paths.

Opposite: The residential towers are strategically located to respond to the prevailing winds for natural ventilation.

Camadas de paisagem são descascadas para abrigar programas públicos.O plano de solo torna-se ativo com canchas esportivas, áreas de descanso, e caminhos de bosque.

Oposto: As torres residenciais são estrategicamente localizadas para responder aos ventos dominantes para ventilatilação natural.

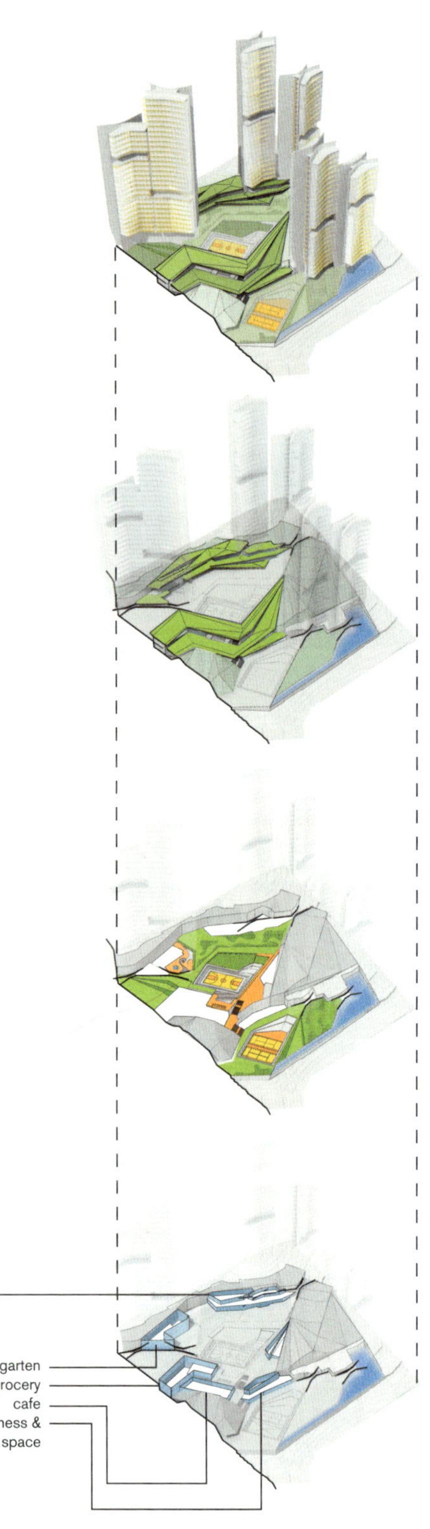

COMBINED LANDSCAPE

–Dry Season

THIN GROUND

–Thin layers which defin courtyards at second level creating semi-public park which meanders through the residential towers.

–During the rainy season, this layer acts as a channel for rainwater runoff which flows to the collection ponds below.

THICK GROUND

–Continuous landscape connects courtyard communities.

–Water collection ponds

–Themed athletic zones

–Playground

AMENITIES

–Public amenities and community zones give identity to each courtyard and allow for social mixing throughout the development.

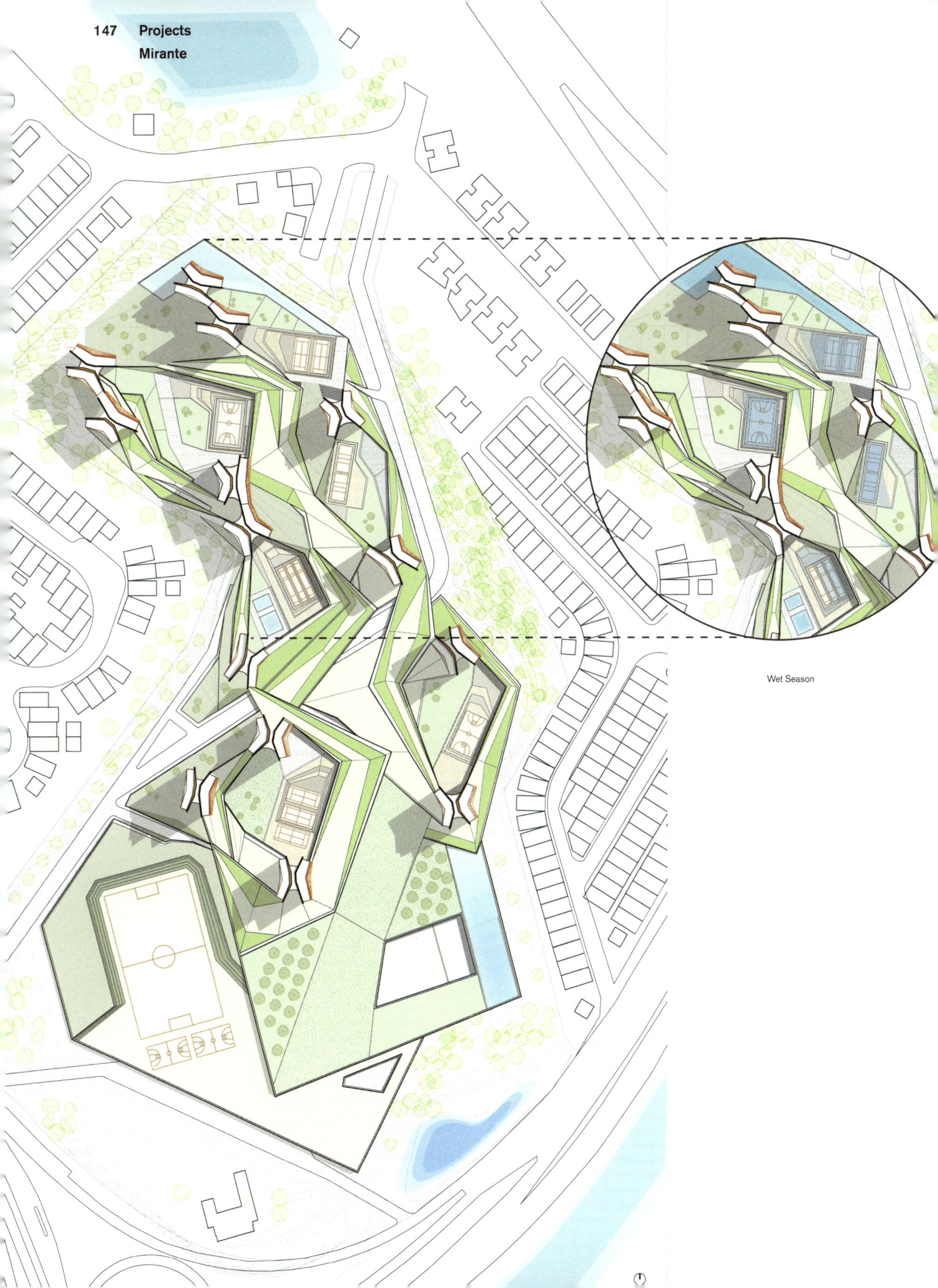

Wet Season

During the wet season, water is channeled through the landscape and collected in large retaining ponds. As the rains lessen, the water is filtered and used for on-site irrigation.

Opposite: Colored panels activate the façades and subtly change their hues from tower to tower.

Durante a estação úmida, a água é canalizada através da paisagem e recolhida em grandes lagoas de retenção. Quando as chuvas diminuem, a água é filtrada e utilizada para a irrigação do local.

Oposto: Painéis coloridos ativam a fachada e sutilmente mudar seus tons de torre a torre.

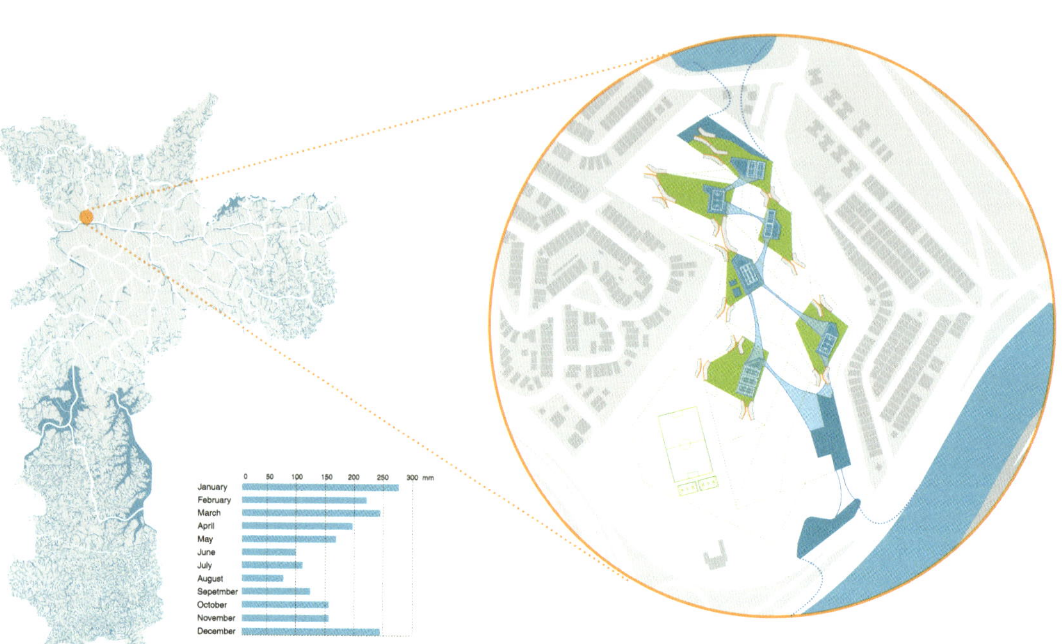

Large courtyards transform from wet to dry with the changing seasons.
Pátios grandes transformam-se de molhados a secos, com a mudança das estações.

STUDIO REVIEW DISCUSSION

RESUMO DO DEBATE NO ESTÚDIO

Opposite, first row from left: Patrick Bellew, Rob Rogers, Andy Bow, Audrey Matlock, Cathleen McGuigan, and Annabelle Selldorf.
Second row from left: Deborah Berke, Robert A.M. Stern.
Oposto, primeira fileira da esquerda: Patrick Bellew, Rob Rogers, Andy Bow, Audrey Matlock, Cathleen McGuigan, and Annabelle Selldorf.
Segunda fileira da esquerda: Deborah Berke, Robert A.M. Stern.

The following are excerpts from the studio reviews throughout the semester, organized thematically.

THE LEGACY OF BRAZILIAN MODERNISM AND SUSTAINABILITY

General Comments

Claire Weisz Many of you took on the challenge of addressing the future of Modernism's legacy in Brazil both in terms of the environment and the rising demand for housing. The most successful projects were the ones that engaged the section as a tool to navigate the topography and resolve programmatic adjacencies. My sense is that the projects wanted to achieve a degree of economy while maintaining a sense of place. The sectional schemes accomplished this both in building and in the master plan.

Patrick Bellew In terms of the influence of Brazilian Modernism on many of the proposals, it is important to understand that although these may be successful Modernist buildings, in most instances they are not great environmentally—so you must push them forward fifty years. Modernism celebrated the new air-conditioning systems, and the challenge for engineers was to see how much cooling could be pumped into the building. Now we know that this is not the right solution and that you have to do it in a different way.

When we look at the hierarchy of spaces in a project, it all starts with the master plan. How do you orient the buildings and distribute the program? Once you have established the overall organization, you must look at how to open up the architecture. How do you design the fenestration? How do you organize the plan so that breezes move through the building? You must think at the scale of the building as well as at the scale of the apartment. Australian architect Glenn Murcutt actually sits in every room to figure out where the most comfortable places are during different times of the day. You have to multiply this exercise by 2,500. If you get it wrong, you will have 5,000 people cursing at the architect just like every schoolchild has done since the 1980s Modernist classroom. The question is how to create livable spaces in a world with much less air-conditioning? As architects, you must embrace these changes. Sustainability and design go hand in hand in the creation of a successful project.

PUBLIC SPACE AND COMMUNITY

General Comments

Peggy Deamer We can identify people playing in parks, but your notion of the community can't just exist at the level of park design. How can we introduce ourselves to the real world where we go shopping with the general public on the same site as a private residential development? At a certain moment, there is a separator—however the images pretend we can be within the larger context—and, at a certain point, we know we're separate from the context.

Cathleen McGuigan The main issue for me is how to address the concern for security so that the project does not become an island in São Paulo. The most challenging and interesting aspect of this project is what happens on the ground plane through the definition and engagement of public spaces.

Peggy Deamer In what way can a project control its territory while maintaining a sense of publicness? If you decide to approach the site as a secure private development, you must admit the project is not just an island. It will be seen by many, and it has edges, which must interact with the public. How can you be a good neighbor in this way? Certainly, quality architecture is one solution. This site is highly visible in São Paulo, and there is an opportunity to look at new sustainable models of architecture and development that could be identifiable in a positive way for the city.

Audrey Matlock I would like to address three points: variety, hierarchy, and security. The variety of schemes was extraordinary and led to very inventive solutions. The most successful projects established a spatial hierarchy, including the relationships between public and private, between open space and edge, and between building typologies. The most successful projects were based on an understanding of the multiple scales of public space. Finally, I find the issue of security very curious. I have not visited São Paulo, but I have been to places such as Kazakhstan where security is a big concern. I am not sure it is as much of an issue of necessity and ownership as it has been stressed today. The notion of keeping people out is the antithesis of community, and how you resolve this contradiction within the project is absolutely key. Are you creating a compound, or are you creating an integral part of the city?

Andy Bow What is the DNA of São Paulo, and what can you learn from it? You must establish a hierarchy to promote a sense of community and capture the spirit of Brazil. I would ask everyone to draw an axon of the first three levels at the base of their schemes, because it is the public space and community programs that make this project. Education and culture are incredibly important to a development like this and give life to the community. As students, you must push and challenge the program to be sustainable and forward-thinking.

Tom Farrell We have discussed the development requirements of density and parking, but a good developer realizes that great public spaces, sense of place, and landscape are essential to successful projects.

THE LEGACY OF BRAZILIAN MODERNISM

Jardim Brasileiro by Lis Cena

Audrey Matlock This project makes a very convincing argument for how a suburban situation can be very urban. You have created a texture that is vertical as opposed to planar; the layers of different texture of hard and soft surfaces and of private and public spaces as well as the way you have woven them together into a set of environmental circumstances is very strong.

Sean Griffiths I'm interested in this idea of context in Brazil. When I look at the context in Jardim Brasiliaro, there is an entirely different tradition of architecture surrounding it—a sort of Portuguese Baroque. In some ways this Modernist project is a historicist scheme, because it looks like a Le Corbusier aesthetic. Le Corbusier's 1930s tower in Rio looks very much like this project. Was there any sense of extending or challenging this tradition of Modernism in Brazil? And, if you had a project in Bloomsbury, London, would you be doing Georgian Classicism?

Robert A.M. Stern You have to realize that this Modernism is a known language, and you're using it very well, but you can't pretend that it's a new thing. The point is to have a methodology, not just a taste.

Claire Weisz Can I misread your project a bit? You are creating a language of building fragments, rather than a complete picture. If anything, you are interested in thinking that an architecture of building fragments—including the strategies on your façade and the collage quality of the landscape fragments—allow for a moving forward of the language of Modernism and climate in order to transform it into something particular that feels like a place.

Annabelle Selldorf This is a place in which people can move about as opposed to an image in which there is just one person lounging in a chair. This seems to me to be a place where communities can happen, and I find that very, very touching, aside from all the practical considerations you give to the climate, the views, the topography, and so on. More than anything, this project is demonstrating process.

Andy Bow This is a very historicist project and therefore encourages a very open debate. The images you showed of the Modernist gardens in Brazil are beautiful, and your handling of the garden at the base is very beautiful. I could just about buy that it's Brazilian—it's got Brazilian gardens. What I would have longed to see is double-height gardens in the sky. Every apartment has access to private outdoor space, but the vertical surfaces are a wee bit soulless and could use more of an interest in the individual. Brazil is a very flamboyant country. If this project were sited under the sullen skies of northern Scotland, I would be horrified, but I would love to see more landscape. You knew you were opening up an interesting critical debate about Modernism.

PHASING

Bandeirantes Arts District by Rebecca Garnett

Claire Weisz How do you create a project—at this scale and to be built by a single entity—to become more than a development?

Audrey Matlock Your question about the phasing is interesting. I think there were one or two projects that had distinct units that incorporated components of outdoor space, commercial space, and living space that one could

From back left: Patrick Bellew, Peggy Deamer, Tom Farrell, and Rob Rogers.

Da parte de trás a esquerda: Patrick Bellew, Peggy Deamer, Tom Farrell, and Rob Rogers.

build and say, "Here's a phase that is self-sustaining until the next phase is built." By and large, most of the schemes are successful when viewed in completion, but one must consider the project's success in phases as well. In many of the schemes, the large central-park component further complicates the way in which the project could successfully be constructed. In each proposal, one must think about the success of the first phase. If you start building on the upper portion of the site, would the built result be strong enough to have people want to live there before the next phase is built?

Katherine Farley A successful project would have to be done in phases—you couldn't possibly build it all at once because you would be cannibalizing your own market, competing with yourself. In one single phase you might sell in the neighborhood of four hundred units, and then when you get sixty percent of that pre-sold, you might start your second phase. Based on the success of the marketing campaign, you could have rolling construction, which would no longer be defined by phases. You must think of the phases as marketing chunks. If the marketing is not going well, you still have to complete that chunk, and it will need to have the resources and amenities that will sustain it as a community until the next portion is sold and built. In the projects that propose central parks, you might build the park in a provisional configuration that can be added to over time.

Audrey Matlock Would you build the cultural center early on?

Katherine Farley For a development like this, it is essential to have a "there" there, or else it becomes banal. Because of the limited access, the project must synchronize its construction phases. As Tom Farrell would say, start building at the top—don't build your Park Avenue apartments and then have concrete trucks roaring past 24/7. One of the challenges of high-density high-rises at the top is that you can't build fifty percent of this project all in one go. The question of how you provide parking for those units is a practical one that has to shape the solution.

Patrick Bellew The paradox is that, in many projects, if you ignore the phasing logistics, you allow for a hierarchy of access to sunlight. Some of the most successful schemes accomplished this. By creating typological zones with strategic spacing, the low-rise, mid-rise, and high-rise units can all have access to sunlight. It is very democratic in the way that the scale responds. Quite an interesting paradox, because it means that the minute you try to phase the design, you actually confront that paradox in a big way.

SCALE AND THE GROUND PLANE
Bandeirantes Arts District by Rebecca Garnett

Annabelle Selldorf In the long site section there is a tiny little development on one end and a gargantuan one on the other end, suggesting a lack of decision about what it is you are actually making. The plan does not have the priorities and the layering. Cities such as Berlin create an enormous amount of units with ten-story buildings that have very large garden courtyards. The site is big enough to warrant that kind of approach and could help you provide density so that you have free area to actually make urban space for the community. There needs to be more of a knitting of the space and more desire for urban public space.

Peggy Deamer This project has a consistent way in which the buildings come down to the ground or don't—that is, there is an emphasis on the openness of a territory that weaves them all together. They come to the ground so confidently. They purport to be contextual even if they are actually not. But there is also a scale, a texture of the façade as it meets the ground, even though what's above changes its scale and program.

Claire Weisz This strategy does not seem to provide a reasonable trade-off for what you get: low-rise, single-family terraced houses. The plan needs to be so dense, but it is just clogging up the bottom of the site and needs more gardens for people.

Andy Bow By retaining the existing buildings and then overlaying another geometry, all sorts of interesting things happen. All these wee bits have the potential to unfold and be really sophisticated little bits of city. But the point about Berlin and Vienna is that they are eight stories high. Personally, I have never liked standing beside a big slab block that's sixteen stories high. I don't mind standing next to towers in parks, but when you stand next to an eight-story-high object, it is a big object. If you then multiply it two or three times in your head, it becomes a different scale altogether. Years ago, I used to do master plans and went for the big idea. However, more and more and more and more and more in our office now, we just talk so much about the spaces we really like and why we like them. With a bit more landscaping, I could genuinely imagine that's the nicest walk of all the schemes we've seen so far. But if you also had a bit of "urban blockness" in here, it could inform the whole site plan. The problem with the Modern strategy is that so many towers are in close proximity—they're all suffocating each other.

Audrey Matlock With the mid-rise project, the proportions are right. Many people have been fascinated with the idea of lifting up the skirt and having the urban space flow under the building, and Bandeirantes Arts District is very successful way. The spaces, like the steps, actually become an urban space with shade.

Rob Rogers These spaces work because they are both specific and ambiguous—they are at the scale of the whole complex. In the little moments of green space, I can imagine fifteen or two people. What is important for the ground plane is the density of the landscape fabric and what it can do in terms of space-making at that three-feet-high scale.

LANDSCAPE

Mirante by Eliza Higgins

Claire Weisz The landscape strategy for this project is the first one we've seen in which the landscape is supposed to be filling a purpose far beyond the scale of the site. It is addressing something that is not only seasonal but actually has a real connection, potentially, to the river, which is now dry half the time and not recognizable as a river. You are looking at a piece of landscape that isn't just local. If that's the big draw of this iconic, hardworking landscape, I wonder why all the buildings have to be the same. You are treating these building as infrastructure. They have a light touch on the landscape, they are providing the right number of units, and they're feeding the spaces. I feel like that's the right argument, but are these the right buildings for that argument?

Andy Bow One universal is that people love parks, from the Parc Citroën in Paris, the High Line in New York City, and Foreign Office's project in Yokohama. People love when landscapes can be sculpted to celebrate nature. Mirante highlights the changing seasons by using landscape to form a central spine where, at different times of the year, it transforms into retaining ponds and directs the flow of water across the site.

Annabelle Selldorf The architectural gesture in this project is confident, and there is a simple strategy at work to make very diverse spaces. Depending on your placement of the butterfly-shaped buildings, the relation they create to one another provides another dimension.

LATER THOUGHTS ON URBAN INTER-SECTIONS

ÚLTIMOS PENSAMENTOS SOBRE INTERSEÇÕES URBANAS

Opposite: Terrace view from Tishman Speyer's luxury residential building, the Metropolitan (completed 2009).
Oposto: Vista do luxuoso prédio residencial geminado da Tishman Speyer, o Metropolitan (completado em 2009).

Deborah Berke After working on this book and gaining some perspective, I realize that the studio may have been even more productive than I first thought. I now fully appreciate the strength of the students' projects, their insight and risk-taking in both conception and design of a real, complex, for-profit real estate development project on a difficult site in a rapidly changing city. The projects were remarkable in their attention to detail and in the number of aspects of design and social issues addressed. The assignment ranged in scale from designing individual units, including the kitchen layout and access to fresh air, to planning multi-unit buildings and creating an overall planning strategy. Parking and access solutions had to be provided for thousands of cars, and the site plan had to address the constructability of 2,500 housing units as well as the needs of the residents. The studio also contemplated landscape design on a property with a difficult topography and challenging access issues. In the end, the goal was to create a viable, marketable product that would be successful in today's competitive São Paulo real estate environment.

To describe any student project in a phrase minimizes its complexity, its depth, and the thoughtfulness behind the design strategy. However, in looking at how the projects were tackled and what design approaches were taken, some patterns did emerge. A number of students focused on a low-rise or mid-rise solution, providing a striking contrast to the ubiquitous, anonymous towers of São Paulo's new cityscape. Becky Garnett's arts-district scheme preserved the existing abattoir ruin and repurposed it as a creative center in a dedicated arts community. Anja Turowski's complex terraced housing was also low-rise and dense and created an interior world below the structures and extensive green topography above.

Quite a few students took on the high-rises of São Paulo by creating memorable and more architecturally distinguished towers. Lis Cena's towers grew out of his Miesian take on master-planning shaped by environmental concerns. Catherine Anderson Poulin's approach to tower-making included integral high-rise parks to give every resident immediate access to green space, creating in-the-air neighborhoods and highly distinctive façades. Carmel Greer's bold design statement used a signature tower as distinctive advertising for the property itself and proposed race-car site roads in contrast to the city's congested traffic.

The creation of significant park space in the highly dense city was another shared design intent among many of the projects. Hilary Zaic constructed a perimeter necklace of buildings to preserve as parkland the largest possible central open space. Eliza Higgins made boomerang-shaped single-loaded towers with inventive unit plans; the towers to sit in a water park and garden specifically devoted to managing run-off during the rainy season. The small

Opposite: Roberto Candusso, architect, Tishman Speyer developers, Florida Penthouses, São Paulo, Brazil, 2008.
Oposto: Roberto Candusso, arquiteto, Tishman Speyer empreendedores, Florida Penthhouses, São Paulo, Brasil, 2008.

clusters of towers Alejandro Fernandez de Mesa designed were set in a Burle Marx–inspired landscape using linked plazas to create different scales of open spaces and parks in the neighborhood.

Students also investigated unusual building forms. Bradley Baer's mid-rise, dense-slab buildings were twisted and perforated to take advantage of ventilation and the views toward his proposed sports arena. Steve Ybarra completed festive hand drawings that flirted with a Venturi-Scott Brown approach to describing a neighborhood development while pushing the boundaries between high-rise and single-family detached housing.

The students benefited from the vast real estate development experience and architecture background of Katherine Farley as well as (I hope) my years of teaching design and growing knowledge of what drives successful urban development projects. However, there is no doubt we learned just as much from each student and their varied and adventurous approaches as they did from us.

We owe a huge and appreciative thanks to Noah Biklen for his superb teaching and focused design criticism throughout the semester and to Nate Shanok for his spirited introduction and ongoing emphasis on the perils and pleasures of real estate development.

I would also like to thank Katherine Farley and her team at Tishman Speyer for their generosity of time and resources, both in New York City and Brazil. It was a significant experience for all the students to be exposed to a developer who values architecture and the creative process.

Finally, Katherine and I would like to thank Edward Bass for his foresight in creating The Edward P. Bass Distinguished Visiting Architecture Fellowship, which made this studio possible.

—Deborah Berke, professor, Yale School of Architecture

BIOGRAPHIES

First row, from left: Andy Bow, Cathleen McGuigan, and Robert A.M. Stern.
Second row, from left: Deborah Berke, Katherine Farley.
Third row, from left: Catherine Anderson Poulin, and Carmel Greer.
Primeira fileira, da esquerda: Andy Bow, Cathleen McGuigan, e Robert A.M.Stern
Segunda fileira, da esquerda: Deborah Berke, Katherine Farley.
Terceira fileira, da esquerda: Catherine Anderson Poulin, e Carmel Greer.

Patrick Bellew is the founding principal of Atelier Ten, environmental engineers based in London and New York City. In 2010, he was the Eero Saarinen Visiting Professor at the Yale School of Architecture, where he has been a visiting lecturer since 2001. He has taught at the Architectural Association, the Bartlett School of Architecture, the University of Reading, and De Montfort University, Leicester. His work at Atelier Ten has gained international recognition for his expertise in sustainable strategies and environmental integration systems. Bellew is a trustee of the U.K. Green Building Council and has received the Royal Designer for Industry award in 2010 as well as the Happold Medal in 2008. In 2004, he was elected a fellow of the Royal Academy of Engineering, London.

Andy Bow is a senior partner at Foster + Partners. Since joining the office in 1996, he has managed the design teams for numerous high-profile projects, both in London and abroad. He has lectured and taught at over thirty schools of architecture and has been a RIBA External Examiner at the Barlett School of Architecture for the last eight years. In 2010, he was the Eero Saarinen Visiting Professor at the Yale School of Architecture. In 2000, he was a judge of the RIBA Bronze and Silver student medals. Bow studied architecture at the Mackintosh School of Architecture in Glasgow.

Peggy Deamer is a principal in the firm Deamer Studio. She is a professor at the Yale School of Architecture, where she teaches design and history/theory. She has taught at the Cooper Union, the University of Kentucky, Barnard College, Columbia University, and Princeton University. Her articles have appeared in *Assemblage, Praxis, Perspecta,* and *Drawings/Buildings/Text.* Her seminar and studio at Yale were published in the book *Millennium House* (The Monacelli Press, 2004). She was the co-editor of *Re-Reading Perspecta* and *Building (in) the Future: Recasting Labor in Architecture* (MIT Press 2010). She received her master's degree in architecture and a Ph.D. from Princeton University.

Sean Griffiths is a director and co-founder of Fashion Architecture Taste (FAT), an art-architecture practice based in London. Griffiths has taught and lectured at institutions around the world including the University of Westminster. He has written articles for CABE and RIBA and has contributed to books, journals, and magazines internationally. Griffiths studied architecture at Manchester Polytechnic and the Polytechnic of Central London. In 2008, he and his partners at FAT taught a Bass studio and in 2010 returned as visiting professors.

Vanessa Grossman is an architect, who also holds a degree from School of Architecture and Urban Planning of the University of São Paulo. She has a Master's degree in the history of architecture from the Paris 1 Panthéon-Sorbonne University. She is currently a Ph.D. candidate in history, theory, and criticism of architecture at Princeton University, where she is pursuing a research on the intersections between politics, architecture, and urbanism both in postwar France and in Brazil. She is the author of the book *A arquitetura e o urbanismo revisitados pela Internacional*

Situacionista (São Paulo: Annablume/FAPESP, 2006). Her work has appeared in *L'architecture d'Aujourd'hui, AMC, Archistorm, Area,* and *Pidgin.*

Tom Farrell is a senior managing director at Tishman Speyer and, over the past sixteen years, has had a leadership role in the development of high-rise projects, including the North Tower in São Paulo, the Hearst Tower in New York City, and the redevelopment of retail and public spaces at Rockefeller Center. He sits on the boards of the New York Building Congress and the ACE Mentor Program of Greater New York. Farrell is a licensed professional engineer and has a bachelor's degree in civil engineering from Manhattan College, where he serves on the board of trustees.

Audrey Matlock is the founder of Audrey Matlock Architect, based New York City and Sag Harbor, N.Y. Her office specializes in residential, cultural, and corporate projects both locally and abroad. Her firm has been recognized for design excellence by the American Institute of Architects, the Architectural League of New York, the International Interior Design Association, and the Society of American Registered Architects. Prior to establishing her own practice in 1993, Matlock worked at Skidmore, Owings & Merrill as well as Perkins + Will, where she was director of design. She has a master's degree from the Yale School of Architecture.

Cathleen McGuigan is an architectural critic, cultural journalist, and teacher. In addition to being a longtime contributor to *Newsweek,* her articles have appeared in *The New York Times Magazine, Smithsonian, Rolling Stone,* and *Harper's Bazaar.* In spring 2011, she was named Editor in Chief of *Architectural Record* magazine. She is an adjunct professor at the Graduate School of Journalism at Columbia University and was a Loeb Fellow at the Harvard University School of Design. McGuigan received her bachelor's degree in the arts from Brown University. She was a Poynter Fellow at Yale in Spring 2011.

Rob Rogers began his architectural partnership with Jonathan Marvel in 1992. Prior to RMA, Rogers worked at I. M. Pei & Partners, where he contributed to projects including the Grande Louvre, in Paris, and the Bank of China, in Hong Kong. Rogers has taught design studios at Pratt Institute, Columbia University, Harvard University, Parsons School of Design, and Washington University. He is a national peer for the U.S. General Services Administration's Design Excellence Program and serves on numerous state and local professional organizations. Rogers received a bachelor's degree in the arts and a bachelor's degree in architecture from Rice University, and he received a master's degree in design studies from the Harvard Graduate School of Design.

Annabelle Selldorf is principal of the New York City-based firm Selldorf Architects. Her practice, founded in 1988, specializes in cultural and art-related projects, including the Neue Gallerie New York: Museum for German and Austrian Art, Gladstone Gallery, also in New York City, and the renovation of the Sterling and Francine Clark Art

Institute, at Williams College, Massachusetts. She received her bachelor's degree in architecture from Pratt Institute and her master's degree in architecture from Syracuse University. She is a fellow of the American Institute of Architects and president of the board of directors of the Architectural League of New York.

Nate Shanok is the managing director of acquisitions for Tishman Speyer and is based in São Paulo, where he directs new investments in Brazil, manages dispositions for the existing portfolio of commercial office investments, and coordinates capital-raising activities. Shanok joined the company in 2005 and was part of its leadership development program, during which he helped underwrite several acquisitions in Boston, Chicago, and Washington, D.C., and assisted with the formation of the Tishman Speyer China Fund. A graduate of Syracuse University, he is a past member of its advisory board international study-abroad program and served on the board of the High School for Leadership and Public Service, in New York City. He received an MBA from the Kellogg School of Management at Northwestern University.

Claire Weisz is a founding partner of WXY architecture + urbanism. Weisz is on the faculty of NYU's Wagner School of Public Policy and has taught at Yale University, Columbia University, and Pratt Institute's School of Architecture. In 2004, she was the co-editor of the *AD* issue "Extreme Sites: Greening the Brownfield." Weisz received her undergraduate degree from the University of Toronto and her master's degree in architecture from Yale.

Image Credits Alejandro Fernandez de Mesa: 044, 046–049, 050–052, 060, 067, 072, 125–131, 160, 162; Anja Turowski: 054,105–111; Bradley Baer: 133–141; Catherine Anderson Poulin: 091–095; Catherine Tighe: 021, 023; Carmel Greer: 119–123; Ciro Miguel: 024–25; Deborah Berke & Partners Architects: 018, 020, 022; Eliza Higgins: 046, 054–059, 062–063, 066, 067, 143–151; Hilary Zaic: 050, 097–103; Jason Schmidt: 019; John Jacobson: 152, 156, 164; Lis Cena: 083–089; MMBB: 027, 037; Noah Biklen: 064, 068–069; Nelson Kon: 028, 031, 033; Prefeitura de São Paulo (prefeitura.sp.gov.br): 056–059, 062; Rebecca Garnett: 054, 075–081; Steve Ybarra: 053, 067, 113–117; Tishman Speyer: 013, 015, 017, 063, 066, 070–071; Umbrella Design: 035.

TRADUCAO NA LINGUA PORTUGUESA

p.003 **ESCOLA DE ARQUITETURA YALE EDWARD P. BASS DISTINGUISHED VISITING ARCHITECTURE FELLOWSHIP INTERSECÇÕES URBANAS: SÃO PAULO KATHERINE FARLEY / DEBORAH BERKE**
Editado por Nina Rappaport, Noah Biklen, e Eliza Higgins

p.005 **ÍNDICE**

p.006 **Sobre Edward P Bass Distinguished Visiting Architecture Fellowship** Em 2003, Edward P.Bass, estudante graduado em 1967 na Yale University, membro da classe de 1972 da Yale School of Architecture, criou esta Fellowship para trazer empreendedores a escola a fim de liderar estudos avançados em colaboração com seus conhecimentos em design. Sr. Bass é um ambientalista que patrocinou o desenvolvimento do projeto Biosfera 2 em Oracle, Arizona, em 1991, e também é o empreendedor responsável pela revitalização contínua da porção central da cidade de Forth Worth, Texas, onde sua praça Sundance Square, que combina restauração com nova construção, transformou um estilo urbano moribundo em um centro regional vibrante. Em todo seu trabalho, Sr. Bass tem sido guiado pela convicção de que arquitetura é uma arte socialmente engajada e esta opera na intersecção de grandes visões e realidades diárias.

A Associação Bass assegura que o currículo escolar reconheça o papel do empreendedor como parte integral do processo de design. A Associação traz empreendedores a Yale para trabalhar lado a lado com educadores e estudantes de arquitetura no estúdio, situando a discussão sobre arquitetura em um discurso abrangente de prática contemporânea. O primeiro estúdio Bass, liderado por Gerald Hines e Louis I. Kahn Visiting Professor Stefan Behnisch, em 2005, foi documentada em *Poetry, Property and Place* (2006). O segundo estúdio Bass, em 2006, que reuniu Stuart Lipton com Saarinem Visiting Professor Sir Richard Rogers ('62), engenheiro Chris Wise, e arquiteto Malcom Smith ('97), foi documentado em *Future-Proofing* (2007). *The Human City* (2008) relata a colaboração do estúdio Yale de Roger Madelin e Bishop Visiting Professor Demetri Porphyrios. *Urban Integration: Bishopgate Goods Yard*, o qual documenta o estúdio liderado por Nick Johnson e a parceria de arquitetura FTA, foi publicada em 2009, e em 2010, o trabalho de estúdio de Charles Atwood e do arquiteto David M. Schwarz's foi publicado em *Learning in Las Vegas*. Com este sendo o sexto livro da série é um prazer apresentar a pesquisa e o trabalho de estúdio liderado pela empreendedora Katherine Farley e professora adjunta da Escola de Arquitetura Yale Deborah Berke, as duas naturais da cidade de Nova Iorque.

p.007 **Prefácio: Robert A.M. Stern, Decano** *Urban Intersections: São Paulo* documenta o sexto trabalho em estúdio entre arquitetos-empreendedores a ser conduzido na Yale, dirigido na primavera de 2010 por Edward P. Bass Visiting Fellow, Katherine Farley, diretora-gerente sênior da Tishman Speyer—uma das empreendedoras mais respeitadas do mundo—e Deborah Berke, professora adjunta na Yale, que desafiou os alunos a projetarem novos loteamentos de complexos de apartamentos em larga escala e de alta densidade em um site—chave no coração de São Paulo, Brasil. Farley, graduada na Brown University e na Harvard School of Design é responsável pelo trabalho da empresa no Brasil e na China bem como seu marketing global. Após o diploma em arquitetura, ela trabalhou para a Ameristone, uma divisão da Turner International e juntou-se à Tishman Speyer em 1984, onde é diretora-gerente desde 1998. Farley também tem contribuído na vida cultural da cidade de Nova Iorque como membro do conselho do Lincoln Center for the Performing Arts desde 2003, e é cadeira do Lincoln Center Development Project. Ela também foi presidente do Real Estate Comittee of the New York Philharmonic Orchestra e membro do conselho do Lincoln Center Theater. Ela serve ao Board of Overseers of the International Rescue Committee e é presidente emeritus do Women in Need.

Deborah Berke fundou sua firma, Deborah Berke & Partners Arechitects, baseada em Nova Iorque, em 1982. Ela recebeu seu diploma em arquitetura pela Rhode Island School of Design e mestrado em planejamento urbano em—urbanismo pelo City University of New York. Em 2005, ela foi premiada com o doutorado honorário pela RISD. Ela tem lecionado arquitetura na Yale desde 1987 e previamente lecionou na University of Maryland, na Rhode Island School of Design, na University of Miami, e The Institute for Architecture and Urban Studies onde foi fellow. Seus projetos incluem diversas residências, renovação e anexo na Yale School of Art, e a conversão do PS122 em um centro de arte em Nova Iorque. Para a Marlboro College, Berke desenvolveu a planta mestre e desenhou o Serkin Center. Ela também preparou a planta do campus para a European College of Liberal Arts em Berlin. A Yale University Press publicou uma monografia sobre seu trabalho em 2009.

Eu gostaria de agradecer à Katherine Farley e a Deborah Berke por sua dedicação ao estúdio. Assim como, eu desejo expressar minha apreciação a Noah Biklen ('03) que ajudou com sua organização, e a Nina Rappaport, diretora de publicações da Yale School of Architecture, com quem Biklen e Eliza Higgins ('10), uma das estudantes no estúdio, co-editaram *Urban Intersections: São Paulo.*

p.008 **Introdução: Nina Rappaport, Noah Biklen, e Eliza Higgins, editores** São Paulo é uma cidade em rápida mudança repleta de novos loteamentos de arranha-céus que contrastam fortemente com o crescimento orgânico das favelas nas encostas, uma disparidade que tornou—se mais evidente pelas conexões limitadas entre os bairros economicamente divididos. Enquanto o design econômico e ambiental tem sido por longa data parte da arquitetura brasileira, só recentemente é que as práticas sustentáveis tem foram aplicadas à escala e à objetivos de desempenho dos novos loteamentos.

O estúdio de Yale, dirigido por Edward P. Bass Distinguished Visiting Architecture Fellow Katherine Farley, diretora administrativa sênior da Tishman Speyer, e a professora da Yale e também arquiteta Deborah Berke, propôs que os estudantes desenhassem um loteamento residencial de classe média. Inicialmente, os estudantes tiveram dificuldade para compreender o projeto, mas o mesmo e as condições culturais de São Paulo ficaram mais claros após uma visita de uma semana à cidade, liderada por Farley no momento em que eles apresentaram seus projetos preliminares à equipe de empreendimento Tishman,baseada em São Paulo. De volta a New Haven, os projetos foram então desenvolvidos em detalhe e foram apresentados no final do prazo a um júri de arquitetos, empreendedores e jornalistas.

Este livro começa com uma conversa entre Katherine Farley e Deborah Berke sobre o empreendimento e design e sobre suas carreiras, seguido por um ensaio, "RMSP", da critica em arquitetura Vanessa Grossman, que escolhe maneiras de entender a história do desenvolvimento da cidade, e aborda desafios enfrentados por arquitetos contemporâneos. Ele é seguido pela documentação dos trabalhos de alunos, começando pela análises do projeto, seguido com seus projetos individuais. Alguns alunos propuseram composições de torres residenciais as quais consideravam segurança, ecologia, amenidades, e a relação com os bairros ao redor. Outros usaram paisagem como uma estratégia de organização, tendo em conta as transformações sazonais, o fluxo de água, ventos predominantes, e circulação como um quadro. Alunos incorporaram elementos arquitetônicos performativos, tais como painéis de sombreamento modular e espaços interiores anulados para criar qualidades distintivas. Acima de tudo, os alunos trabalharam para dar uma forma de projeto ao bairro, analisando os edifícios em relação a novos bairros e serviços comunitários, ou jardins com paisagens topográficas que contrastavam com as características superquadras do Modernismo brasileiro.

O livro termina com trechos da revisão final do júri
final por Patrick Bellew, Andy Bow, Peggy Deamer,
Tom Farrell, Sean Griffiths, Audrey Matlock ('79),
Cathleen McGuigan, Rob Rogers, Annabelle Selldorf,
e Claire Weisz (89), enquanto estes discutiam
empreendimento ético, sustentabilidade e acessibilidade na economia brasileira em constante mudança,
e os comentários finais por Deborah Berke. Os
p.009 editores gostariam de reconhecer o trabalho dos
estudantes que participaram do estúdio e cuja
cooperação foi essencial para este livro: Bradley Baer
('11), Lis Cena ('11), Rebecca Garnett ('10), Carmelo
Greer ('10), Alejandro Fernandez de Mesa ('10), Eliza
Higgins ('10), Catherine Anderson Poulin ('10), Anja
Turowski ('10), Steve Ybarra ('10), e Hilary Zaic ('10).

Também estendemos nossa apreciação ao trabalho de Gabriel Köche Cé e Karini Villarinho Machado que traduziram o livro para o Português. Nosso stalwart editor de cópia David Delp merece reconhecimento bem como as designers gráficas Sarah Gephart e Tracey Chan do mgmt. design, em Nova Iorque por seu trabalho elegante.

p.010 I. O VALOR DO DESIGN: O DIÁLOGO

p.012 **Katherine Farley** e **Deborah Berke** conversam sobre seus trabalhos e ensino com a crítica de arquitetura Nina Rappaport.

Nina Rappaport Katherine, o que lhe inspirou para lecionar arquitetura? Você é formada em arquitetura, mas alguma vez ensinou arquitetura?

Katherine Farley Eu acredito que é importante para os arquitetos não somente aprenderem a desenhar, mas também a construir nossos desenhos. Se o aprendizado de arquitetura não inclui treinamento nas habilidades necessárias para transformar uma idéia de design ultrapassando obstáculos tais como desenvolvimento-e-contrução, então os arquitetos não estarão preparados para construir seus projetos. O objetivo do Studio é expor os alunos a fatores reais que envolvam a execução de um projeto real.

NR Como você se tornou uma pioneira no desenvolvimento imobiliário? Como era quando você começou a trabalhar em uma companhia de empreendimentos?

KF Eu me lembro da minha primeira entrevista, "Nos temos 3, 200 empregados—Gostaria de conhecer a outra mulher?" Aquilo foi uma sacudida, mas também uma grande experiência. Eu acredito que as pessoas que foram os maiores exemplos de vida e inspiração foram as que eu conheci na China. O estilo de negociação na China era mais confortável para mim do que o utilizado nos Estados unidos. Eu aprendi muito somente observando-os trabalhar. Naquele tempo existiam muito mais mulheres no desenho, desenvolvimento e constr-ução nas empresas Norte Americanas—porém não o suficiente—e mais e mais se vê mulheres assumindo posições mais elevadas em empresas internacionais.

NR Deborah, seu trabalho tem sido freqüentemente focado em projetos institucionais e relacionados com arte: Quais são seus projetos atuais e como você os conceitua?

Deborah Berke No exato momento estamos trabalhando em vários projetos interessantes que variam de residências para prédios institucionais relacionados com arte, sendo estes: projeto de artes cênicas em SUNY Fredonia, conservatório de musica na Universidade da Bard, e um prédio para ensino cinematográfico na UNCSA. Estamos também desenhando dois hotéis, nos estados do Arkansas e Ohio, que são parte da expansão da marca "21c Museum Hotel" que começamos a trabalhar anos antes em Louisville, Kentucky. Em Nova Iorque estamos trabalhando em um projeto de arte financiados pelo governo; a renovação extensiva da 122CC, uma antiga escola publica que por muito tempo abrigou projetos de artes como "Mabou Mines and Performance Space 122" e "Painting Space 122," a galerias. Este é um projeto "DDC Design Excellence" e o inicio das obras esta programado para começar este ano. Estamos também dando continuidade ao nosso trabalho na Escola Européia de Artes Liberais em Berlim onde o Campus no bairro Pankow (antiga Berlim Oriental) é composto de várias antigas embaixadas. Nosso plano propõe uma maneira de conectar os prédios distintos para form ar um campus, bem como construir adições e novas estruturas para atender às suas necessidades. Estamos agora avançando com o primeiro destes edifícios.

p.014 **NR** É interessante verificar como alguns dos empreendedores vem ensinando nos Studios da "Yale Bass Fellowship" nos últimos quatro anos—como por exemplo Roger Madelin, da Argent, em Londres—utilizando uma certa filosofia para orientar seus funcionários. Por exemplo, o conceito da empresa Madelin's é "Princípios para uma Nova Cidade Humana." Existe uma filosofia que a Tishman Speyer usa para construir projetos ao redor do mundo, em lugares como Índia, Brasil e China? Qual é a sua visão para o desenho urbano em culturas diversas?

KF Sim, nós temos uma filosofia: a excelência. Desenvolvemos edifícios que representam a excelência, uma definição que muda tanto ao longo do tempo e por causa do mercado. Acreditamos que um edifício de alta qualidade é o último a sofrer em uma recessão e o primeiro a se recuperar. Edifícios deste calibre atraem os melhores inquilinos e tem o fluxo de renda mais protegido. Contratamos executivos tops de linha que estão comprometidos com a excelência em nossos edifícios, nosso povo e nossos padrões de profissionalismo. Nossos prédios não têm a mesma aparência em todo mercado. Cada edifício é projetado para atender as exigências da população do mercado local. Nós desenvolvemos o que é considerado o top de linha em qualquer mercado em que estamos trabalhando. Por exemplo, no Brasil a quinze anos atrás o mercado local definia um espaço de Classe A de uma certa maneira. Quando nós construímos o nosso primeiro prédio no Brasil, o mercado local começou a se referir a ele como um espaço de Classe AA.

NR De quais projetos você se orgulha mais?

KF Eu diria que do Messeturm, em Frankfurt, projetado por Helmut Jahn, que foi o nosso primeiro projeto internacional e era também o edifício mais alto da Europa na época. A Torre Norte, nosso primeiro projeto no Brasil, projetado por um escritório local chamado Botti Rubin Arquitetos, que definiu o novo padrão de qualidade do qual eu mencionei anteriormente. Desde então, terminamos os dois primeiros "green projects" na América do Sul: um projetado por um arquiteto local, Aflalo e Gasperini Arquitetos, e o segundo é um belo projeto no Rio projetado pela KPF.

NR Como você incorpora a sustentabilidade para os projetos de grande dimensão? Seria isto parte do seu padrão de aprimoramento?

KF Como empresa, entendemos que o mundo da sustentabilidade está evoluindo, e nós pensamos que estamos na linha de frente na abordagem destas questões. Muitas coisas, a partir da tecnologia até a disposição dos inquilinos a pagar por isso, estão evoluindo. Provavelmente, o edifício mais importante que concluímos foi o Hearst Tower, de Norman Foster, que foi o primeiro edifício LEED Gold, em Manhattan. Embora eu não tenha tido uma participação muito próxima a esse projeto, me orgulho muito dele.

NR Como você tem utilizado a sua experiência em arquitetura nos seus projetos? Por exemplo, como você orienta o desenho de um projeto?

p.016 **KF** O desenvolvimento é feito de escolhas. Dado que não exista projeto com orçamento ilimitado, estamos engajados em um processo de priorização de elementos de desenho e escolha daqueles que serão mais significativos para o projeto arquitetônico e simultaneamente para os fins de mercado. Minha formação como arquiteta tem sido inestimável nesse processo.

NR Deborah, a ocasião deste Studio tem referência com seus trabalhos mais recentes com empreendedores focados em resultados. Como você continua a manter standars de design os ideais sob esta restrição?

DB Estou trabalhando com empreendedores em projetos em Nova York, e para o grupo "21c Museum Hotels", com um hotel construído em Louisville, Kentucky, e mais três em andamento. Eu gosto quando os desafios apresentados por um orçamento justo falam mais alto nos diálogos que ajudam a moldar o trabalho. Essa relação guia o processo de design em uma maneira diferente do diálogo no trabalho institucional. Eu mantenho os padrões por ser capaz de argumentar com sucesso o papel do desenho na definição de "marca" e na criação de valores.

NR Na sua opinião o que define um bom empreendedor? Você está interessada no lado comercial de projetos de desenvolvimento?

DB Não, mas eu não quero dizer isso de uma forma displicente. Eu entendo que os números têm que funcionar, e isso é uma restrição positiva, especialmente com um "bom" empreendedor. Um bom empreendedor não necessariamente coloca mais dinheiro em um projeto, mas entende a necessidade de fazer escolhas orçamentais sugeridas pelo desenho.

NR Você já surpreendeu algum empreendedor por incorporar elementos de desenho mais elegantes e ao mesmo tempo reduzir os custos?

DB O nosso edifício na 48 Bond Street, em Nova York é um grande exemplo. É um bonito edifício no qual todas as unidades foram vendidas antes das unidades do prédio da competição do mesmo bloco ter as suas, aprovando o modelo. O empreendedor queria trabalhar com um arquiteto porém mantendo o pensamento em resultados financeiros. Nós vendemos a ele a grande idéia do projeto, que era a natureza da fachada. Em determinado momento acho que isso é verdade em todo o meu trabalho, eu prefiro gastar um pouco de dinheiro em algumas áreas do projeto e gastar muito mais em outras áreas, ao invés de gastar quantidades modestas em todas as áreas. Isso foi uma estratégia que testamos na Bond Street, com a fachada, a piscina e em certos aspectos dos apartamentos—escolhemos algumas áreas para investir mais e outras menos.

NR Katherine, o que você considera um bom relacionamento entre você e os arquitetos, e como você conduz o projeto? Que parte do processo você mais gosta?

KF Eu acho que o processo de desenho é mais bem sucedido quando você tem um arquiteto experiente e talentoso, que possua um forte ponto de vista mas que também compreende que um projeto de sucesso tem muitos outros aspectos que devam ser acomodados além do simples e puro desenho por
p.019 um lado você não quer um arquiteto que diz: “Apenas me diga o que fazer e vou fazê-lo”, mas por outro lado você não quer um arquiteto que é dogmático e acha que só existe uma maneira de resolver um problema. É muito empolgante fazer parte de uma equipe que representa vários tipos de conhecimentos e que se junta para enfrentar os desafios do empreendimento, com o objetivo comum de desenvolver um grande projeto.

NR Como você seleciona arquitetos e monta uma equipe local para projetos, como a Torre Norte, no Brasil, projetado por Botti Rubin Arquitetos? Quais as vantagens de ter uma equipe local para projetos de empreendimento?

KF Quando abrimos os escritórios no exterior nos criamos a equipe “Tishman Speyer” que é essencialmente local. Eles vem da cultura local e falam a língua local, mas também são parte da cultura global e profissional da “Tishman Speyer.” A empresa toda é consistente com as melhores práticas em desenho e questões técnicas. Nós trabalhamos duro para ser uma empresa global e não apenas uma franquia regional. O Brasil, por exemplo, inicialmente usou uma combinação de arquitetos locais e internacionais e aceitou um certo grau de redundância no início para ter certeza de que poderíamos oferecer a qualidade internacional que nossos inquilinos esperam de nós. Como nós ganhamos experiência no Brasil, temos cada vez mais utilizado arquitetos locais, embora muitas vezes ainda temos a participação de arquitetos internacionais.

NR Qual é o seu papel nestes projetos no exterior? Você influência a escolha do arquiteto e do local?

KF Ao longo dos anos o meu papel tem variado, mas incluiu em vários momentos tanto a inicialização quanto a responsabilidade geral regional para a Alemanha, França, Argentina e Índia. Hoje eu sou responsável por nossos negócios no Brasil e na China. Neste papel eu estou profundamente envolvida em todos os aspectos do negócio, incluindo a aquisição do lote e a seleção do arquiteto, entre outras coisas. Antes de escolher um arquiteto, discutimos nossas idéias com a equipe local e o departamento de design e construção em nossa sede em Nova York. Com o projeto em desenvolvimento, a equipe local trabalha diariamente com o arquiteto, e eu freqüentemente confiro o design e revisões gerais do projeto. Em nossas análises de projeto, os especialistas em empréstimos, marketing, design, construção e gestão de propriedades comentam o desenho considerando todos os aspectos de desenvolvimento, incluindo a construção, viabilidade e custo.

NR Deborah, por que os hotéis 21c tem sido tão bem sucedido financeiramente e em termos de estratégia de design?

DB Este hotel é uma experiência incrível. Os quartos e os espaços públicos são projetados com cuidado. Nós não somos arquitetos de hotéis, por isso olhamos para o interior com olhos diferentes. Os proprietários não são empreendedores de hotéis e nós não temos um modelo de desenho pronto de hotéis, e eles também não queriam um. O primeiro objetivo deles era para o hotel contribuir no renascimento da cidade de Louisville, Kentucky. O sucesso foi uma surpresa e um prazer. A integração da arte no hotel é
p.021 absolutamente verdadeira, não é uma estratégia de marketing ou uma idéia de “marca comercial”. Os donos são verdadeiros colecionadores de arte e querem compartilhar sua coleção. Esta visão específica infunde a experiência do hotel e a arte é real. Acho que as pessoas intuitivamente entendem isso.

NR Como você está lidando com as mudanças no ambiente econômico? E com isso em mente, como você aconselharia os estudantes de arquitetura?

KF Em tempos de crise econômica é mais importante do que nunca para os alunos compreenderem as outras perspectivas que entram em jogo no desenvolvimento de edifícios. Um arquiteto bem-sucedido precisa ser hábil em outras áreas além do puro desenho e compreender a relação entre desenho e questões financeiras, técnicas, de sincronismo e até mesmo política e macroeconômica. O objetivo do Studio também foi para ajudar os arquitetos a compreenderem como priorizar estas questões de forma que os aspectos mais significativos do projeto sejam preservados, mesmo em momentos de pressão econômica.

NR O que foi mais desafiante em relação ao lote escolhido para o o estúdio?

DB O projeto está em uma área complexa, com uma significativa inclinação e um edifício histórico não-muito-interessante que precisa ser salvo. A área faz fronteira com uma variedade de diferentes bairros. Algumas das questões de projeto incluem a definição de que tipo de lugar este será abordado por diferentes áreas, bem como apresentar soluções para o difícil acesso. O quadro global—que é mais interessante—é que este é um projeto residencial de classe média. Embora o problema de habitação dos pobres nos países emergentes é de enorme importância, não é algo que você possa resolver em um estúdio de empreendimentos. É uma questão governamental. Mas estamos pedindo aos alunos para olhar primeiro o componente habitacional e segundo adicionar múltiplos usos. O que você pode adicionar ao programa que é apropriado para a esta área da cidade e quais são suas aspirações? E se você fizer habitação, o que se pode adicionar a isto—instalações esportivas, uma escola, uma biblioteca? Não podemos pensar nos tipos de atrativos americanos para venda de habitação. Em vez disso, perguntamos: o que vai torná-lo um lugar melhor para viver? A idéia do Studio não foi desenhar um projeto completo de unidades residenciais, mas sim estimular os alunos a pensarem sobre a natureza da comunidade a qual estão criando.

KF Eles foram avaliados em como resolver o problema de design e também como esta solução responde a uma variedade de desafios de desenvolvimento, incluindo a sustentabilidade, comercialização, e viabilidade de construção. Também fizemos uma versão simplificada de um exercício para cálcular custos, e os alunos aprenderam a resolver as questões comerciais do mundo real. Por exemplo, eles viram que a escolha de uma parede cara de cortina de vidro torna difícil alcançar a classificação de sustentabilidade desejada, e um aluguel mais alto seria necessário para que o projeto seja viável comercialmente. As discussões com especialistas de mercado ajudaram a determinar se o valor adicionado por decisoes de projeto seria absorvido no
p.023 mercado pelos inquilinos suficientemente para justificar essa escolha. À medida em que pesaram as opções, nós discutimos o valor mais alto dos edifícios chamados "troféus", onde os inquilinos pagam aluguel mais alto para um edifício com um design excelente.

NR A maioria dos outros estúdios de empreendimentos tem como foco o planejamento de estruturas para grandes áreas de desenvolvimento, com os alunos desenhando apenas a concepção arquitetônica dos edifícios em um esquema mais esquemático e menos detalhado. O quanto você gostaria de ver prédios completamente projetados entrarem dentro destes conceitos?

DB O estúdio passou pela fase do plano-mestre rapidamente para em seguida chegar a uma menor parte do projeto em que os alunos poderiam desenvolver prédios. Eu estava interessada nas áreas de intersecção dos programas comunitários e residenciais. Os alunos não tinham a concepção de cada unidade, mas foi interessante ver o impacto do plano-mestre em cada instalação e qual é a relação entre a comunidade e o edifício.

NR O que você esperava que os alunos aprendessem e que normalmente não seria ensinado em um Estúdio liderado por um arquiteto?

DB Eu acho que o vai-e-vem entre as disciplinas demonstraram as negociações entre custos e design. É importante que os alunos compreendam as pressões decorrentes dos empreendimentos: isto irá torná-los melhores arquitetos e também contribuirá mais profundamente para o ambiente construído como um todo.

p.024 II. A CIDADE EM DESENVOLVIMENTO: SÃO PAULO

p.028 RMSP: REGIAO METROPOLITANA DE SÃO PAULO

Vanessa Grossman, critica em arquitetura e história, discute os desafios de infraestrutura e desenvolvimento em São Paulo oferecendo um contexto para o studio.

"Um amigo me disse recentemente que tinha percorrido a região do Harz, na Alemanha, usando um mapa de rua de Londres, cujas instruções ele seguiu cegamente. Este tipo de brincadeira não é nada além do que um mau começo que poderia resultar em uma construção completa de arquitetura e urbanismo." Aqui, seguindo as idéias do amigo de Guy Debord, vou aterrissar em Paris e usar um de seus mapas a fim de conduzir o leitor para um local do outro lado do Atlântico, a chamada Região Metropolitana de São Paulo (RMSP).

Enquanto à deriva pelas ruas de Paris em 1950, o situacionista Debord passou a acreditar que as cidades têm uma imagem psicogeográficas, com correntes constantes, pontos fixos e vórtices que incentivam a atração ou repulsão de determinadas áreas. Ele desenvolveu as chamadas *"cartas psychogégographiques"*, ou "mapas psicogeográficos", pois a concepção de um mapa de posse de territórios é substituída pela representação de caminhos irregulares, atmosferas e subjetivos desordem. Desintegrando a soberana unidade da cidade, o seu *Guide Psychogéographique de Paris* (Guia Psicográfico de Paris) em 1956 consistiu em uma coleção de fragmentos urbanos de Paris selecionados, representando um espaço urbano subjetivamente recomposto. No entanto, Debord estava insatisfeito não só com as habilidades cartográficas dos cartógrafos, mas também com trabalho de arquitetos e urbanistas. Os fragmentos representados referiam-se principalmente àqueles em vias de desaparecimento, como consequência da reconstrução de Paris após a Segunda Guerra Mundial. Um dos resultados de tal processo foi a formação dos.

Quase sessenta anos depois, esse processo de urbanização atingiu um estágio de consolidação. Apesar da presença da *Périphérique*—a rodovia que cerca Paris, situada entre a cidade e seus subúrbios—o que é rotulado como "Grande Paris" persiste como uma unidade soberana em termos de sua infraestrutura e até mesmo no "mapa mental" dos seus habitantes. Há diferenças, entretanto, no que diz respeito à qualidade dos seus espaços urbanos, bem como à escala de suas distâncias. No entanto, o mapa do metrô de Paris, por exemplo, oferece a seus usuários um bom senso da Grande Paris como um todo único: suas extensões, limites e acessibilidade.

Se eu me desviei do tema principal deste ensaio, para examinar a representação psicogeográfica da cidade através de seus fragmentos, foi porque o que poderia ser descrito como uma subjetividade situacionista parece se realizar objetivamente em outras localidades do globo, marcadas por diferentes circunstâncias sociopolíticas. Uma destas regiões seria a RMSP, onde fragmentação não é uma abstração mas sim uma condição urbana. Os arquitetos e urbanistas brasileiros Leandro Medrano e Luiz Recamán lêem a formação destes aglomerados urbanos, muitas vezes objeto de projeto e planejamento que são, por outro lado raramente executados, como "um processo infinito de justaposição, descontinuidade e fragmentação, transformando a cidade inteira em um movimento cíclico de produção de valor e segregação."

Na verdade, todo este processo consiste em um desenvolvimento recente, já que a RMSP não existia antes de 1973. A RMSP é constituída por 39 municípios, 38 dos quais são agrupados em torno da capital do estado, São Paulo, e estão direta ou indiretamente polarizados por ela.

p.031 Na verdade, todo este processo consiste em um desenvolvimento recente, já que a RMSP não existia antes de 1973. A RMSP é constituída por 39 municípios, 38 dos quais são agrupados em torno da capital do estado, São Paulo, e estão direta ou indiretamente polarizados por ela.

Isso representa 3,4% do total do território do Estado de São Paulo, com uma área de 8,051 quilômetros quadrados, ou 3,108.508 milhas quadradas, na qual 48,04% da população do estado está concentrada. A RMSP é caracterizada por uma conturbação significativa das áreas pertencentes a municípios diferentes, uma concentração de cerca de 19.7 milhões pessoas, e desenvolvimento de um complexo sistema de centros concentrados de atividades terciárias em vários níveis.

A RMSP passou a se expandir rapidamente sobretudo após a década de 1970, quando um enorme contingente populacional do Nordeste do Brasil, sem recursos para pagar pelo preço da terra urbana, começou a migrar para São Paulo. Esta nova onda migratória deu luz a um processo de crescimento urbano não-orquestrado, marcado por um déficit em todos os sentidos: em termos de habitação social, principalmente caracterizada por auto-construção, em termos de urbanização e infraestrutura, com a formação de *favelas* e *periferias* (os subúrbios), ambas marcadas por um processo de subdivisão da terra clandestino, e em termos de transporte público, complementado pela circulação de vans clandestinas (as chamadas *"peruas"*) que operam em áreas aonde o sistema de transporte oficial ainda não chegou. Se os habitantes das *favelas* representava 1% da população de São Paulo no início da década de 1970, no início da década de 1990 eles representam 20%.

Nesse sentido, pode-se argumentar que arquitetos e urbanistas não projetaram uma parte significativa da RMSP e, consequentemente, descontinuidade territorial, auto-construção e segregação territorial de classes poderiam ser consideradas três de suas características principais. Se as idéias de Kevin Lynch fossem aplicadas em São Paulo, através de um estudo que revelasse como os seus habitantes representam mentalmente o mapa da RMSP, independentemente de sua classe social, este mapa seria indubitavelmente psicogeográfico. Seria de fato um guia para determinadas zonas da RMSP, já que nenhum de seus habitantes tem acesso aos demais fragmentos que compõem o tecido urbano descontínuo desta megacidade.

E ainda assim São Paulo tem sido sucessivamente objeto de planejamento urbano e legislação que nem sempre foram seguidos ou mesmo implementados. O mais recente, o *Plano Diretor Estratégico do Município de São Paulo*, aprovado em Setembro de 2002, em vigor até 2012, tem sido polemicamente discutido e debatido desde a sua aprovação. Um dos primeiros planos urbanísticos estruturais de São Paulo pode ser considerado como exceção a esta regra, já que acabou de fato orientando a expansão metropolitana. Este plano remete à década de 1930, quando Prestes Maia, um dos mais renomados urbanistas e prefeitos da cidade, decidiu abraçar o automóvel em seu *"Plano de Avenidas."* Aquilo que foi concebido como uma solução estrutural acabou gerando alguns dos principais problemas da RMSP, como uma consequência do "casamento" entre um sistema inteiramente baseado no automóvel e a ausência de investimento em transporte público, ambas características das principais cidades brasileiras.

p.032 Além disso, os inúmeros vales, que outrora serviram para drenagem de águas residuais da cidade, foram transformados em vias de grande tráfego. Aos poucos os antigos rios e canais passaram a ser utilizados como estradas, e não como parques ou espaços públicos. Este processo de impermeabilização das áreas com capacidade natural de absorção de água pluvial têm sido agravado pelo fato de que, nas últimas décadas, assentamentos não planejados passaram a ocupar as áreas de nascentes, rios e córregos relacionados a bacias hidrográficas que ainda tiveram seus sistemas de drenagem afetados pelas alterações climáticas. Como consequência, as inundações ainda constituem um dos principais problemas da RMSP.

Em termos de planejamento urbano, desde 1912, a "City of São Paulo Improvements and Freehold Land Company Ltd.", mais conhecida no Brasil como "Cia City", tem sido outra presença forte em São Paulo. Esta companhia, fundada pelo arquiteto francês Joseph Bouvard, juntamente com investidores Franceses, Britânicos e Brasileiros, estava atenta às direções para as quais São Paulo estava se expandindo, especialmente em relação às suas principais atividades e infraestrutura durante as primeiras décadas do século XX. Desta maneira eles transformaram um dos maiores pântanos da cidade—antigas propriedades, então consideradas insalubres e muito úmidas, que a empresa adquiriu de proprietários privados—em um dos bairros mais luxuosos de São Paulo. Foi nestes novos bairros urbanizados, principalmente concebidos para as classes média e alta, que o conceito de cidade-jardim foi introduzido pela primeira vez na América do Sul. Como parte de sua estratégia de urbanização, altamente apoiada pelo governo de São Paulo, a companhia Britânica também prestou serviços complementares essenciais, tais como a provisão de eletricidade e transporte.

Trabalhando para a "Cia City", em 1913, o renomado arquiteto Inglês Barry Parker projetou o *Jardim América*, o primeiro *Bairro Jardim* de São Paulo, não como um bairro residencial, mas como uma "comunidade fechada". Em 1917, o arquiteto redesenhou o layout do *Jardim América*, transformando a sua divisão em enormes lotes em uma divisão estritamente residencial, pontuada por jardins semi-públicos acessíveis através de ruas pitorescas. Esta decisão foi baseada no Decreto Municipal de 1929, que não só proibiu a construção de edifícios não residenciais nesse bairro, mas também estabeleceu a requisição de recuos e alinhamentos. As premissas do Decreto Municipal que passaram a reger os *bairros jardins* podem ser lidas como um prelúdio para os processos de distanciamento social e segregação catalisados no final do século XX, quando a metrópole começou a mostrar um aumento nos índices de criminalidade. Doravante, cercas e câmeras de vigilância substituíram a natureza vista pelos ingleses no início do século como um dispositivo de fechamento, e São Paulo se tornou no fim do século XX a "cidade de muros", descrita pela antropóloga Teresa Caldeira.

O desenvolvimento destas verdadeiras "ilhas" residenciais verdes, dispersas, ainda que estritamente urbanizadas, tirou proveito dos novas vias criadas pelo *Plano de Avenidas* de Prestes Maia. A Cia City também foi responsável pela abertura dessas avenidas, como a antiga Avenida Anhangabaú, hoje chamada Avenida Nove de Julho, bem como a sua extensão em 1930, até o *Jardim América*. Este eixo norte-sul ligando alguns dos bairros-jardins com outras partes da cidade ainda é uma das principais
p.034 avenidas de São Paulo. Assim, se os sucessivos planos urbanísticos de São Paulo foram parcialmente seguidos—como foi o caso do *Plano de Avenidas*—ou jamais implementados, estes fragmentos urbanos planejados poderiam ser interpretados como seus verdadeiros resultados: a sucessão de planos pilotos definiu uma cidade aberta a este tipo de intervenção privada, que se realiza na dimensão do lote urbano.

Por outro lado, o sistema público de transporte em São Paulo não acompanhou este processo de crescimento urbano, acelerado e descontínuo. O Metrô, inaugurado em setembro de 1974, composto por somente quatro linhas (a quinta está ainda no papel) é incapaz de dar conta da escala da RMPS. Seu desenvolvimento, insuficiente, foi resultado da falta de recurso financeiro, o que não é mais o caso. Todavia, o cenário do transporte urbano em São Paulo é marcado pela maciça presença de helicópteros. De acordo com a revista *Veja* (2002), a RMSP tem a maior frota de helicópteros no mundo fora dos Estados Unidos. Esta frota, associada à total ausência de planejamento de trafico aéreo, é responsável pelo fato de que São Paulo tem setenta vezes mais heliportos do que a cidade de Nova Iorque e sete vezes mais do que a combinação dos heliportos em Tókio, Los Angeles, Frankfurt, Londres, Roma, Chicago e Paris. Helicópteros é certamente uma maneira mais efetiva de conectar os fragmentos urbanos da RMSP do que nenhuma outra modalidade de transporte, especialmente em relação ao grande engarrafamento.

Mas conectando o fosso social entre os dois extremos da população da RMSP—usuários de helicópteros de um lado, e de *peruas* do outro— uma nova classe média esta emergindo da reestruturação macroeconômica e de programas de assistência social implementados de forma consistente por recentes administrações governamentais. A última delas conseguiu deslocar aproximadamente trinta milhões de pessoas acima da linha de pobreza no Brasil. Consequentemente, o mercado de consumo interno vem expandido significantemente. Neste novo cenário nacional, com seus inúmeros centros comerciais, shopping centers, e outros serviços, a RMSP representa o principal destino atraindo pessoas de todo o país e do mundo. Na atual ordem global o Brasil ocupa uma nova posição dentro da formação do quarteto BRIC de potências emergentes—Brasil, Rússia, índia e China—em 2009 e São Paulo é definitivamente uma das mais importantes regiões.

Outrora uma grande cidade industrial, a RMSP é hoje uma megacidade global de negócios e serviços. Esta condição vem produzindo empreendimentos caracterizados por uma nova mescla de programas, incluindo parques, hotéis, centros de conferência, e eventos relacionados à moda. Antigas áreas industriais e edifícios históricos, segmentos particularmente localizados nos arredores do centro da cidade, vem se transformando em mercados abertos, uma nova realidade que emerge acompanhada pelo intenso processo de gentrificação que é típico em tal conjuntura. Desde a democratização política no inicio dos anos oitenta, membros dos movimentos de habitação popular tentaram resistir ocupando alguns dos prédios vazios ou abandonados nas áreas centrais da cidade. Grande parte destas ocupações acabou sendo removidas, porém não relocalizadas, o que acabou por intensificar o processo de êxodo em direção às *periferias* da RMSP.

De fato, esta população tem sido empurrada para os assentamentos periféricos da cidade desde os anos setenta, assentamentos caracterizados pela ausência
p.036 de planejamento urbano e por uma "arquitetura sem arquitetos." E é desta forma que se constitui o desenvolvimento da RMSP, marcado pela descontinuidade de seu tecido urbano. E ainda assim, de janeiro de 2010 até dezembro de 2010, empreendedores imobiliários lançaram 67.775 unidades residenciais em São Paulo, enquanto que na segunda cidade mais importante do Brasil—Rio de Janeiro—16.787 foram lançadas no mesmo período. Estes novos empreendimentos urbanos destinados à classe média emergente seguiram a evolução da tendência das "comunidades fechadas" dos *bairros jardins* de 1910, que foram finalmente intensificados por empreendedores imobiliários através dos chamados "condomínios fechados" da década de setenta, como Alphaville, criado pela empresa de construção civil e incorporadora Albuquerque & Takaoka, que o filósofo francês Paul Virilio definiu como um verdadeiro "bunker para as elites". Alphaville consiste em empreendimentos suburbanos altamente protegidos destinados a finalidades tanto industriais, quanto comerciais e residenciais, a última voltada para classes sociais altas. A comunidade foi criada não somente em razão do aumento da violência em São Paulo, como também por conta dos engarrafamentos e do número limitado de parques públicos e de áreas verdes.

Os anos setenta também marcaram o crescimento de empreendimentos urbanos similares, caso do pioneiro *Condomínio Ilha Sul*, também lançado pela Albuquerque & Takaoka, localizado no Alto de Pinheiros, um distrito de classe média alta situado na Zona Oeste de São Paulo. Por causa dos altos preços do mercado imobiliário, *Ilha Sul* é não é um empreendimento horizontal, mas uma estrutura vertical fechada. O empreendimento é composto de seis torres que abrigam um clube com uma piscina interna e duas externas, uma sauna, área para churrasco, playground, uma biblioteca, uma creche, uma boate, inúmeros salões de festas, uma sala de piano e um teatro onde a famosa cantora brasileira Elis Regina já cantou. Trata-se de um conjunto cercado por áreas verdes. Esta nova tipologia urbana, organizada como uma cidade reinventada dentro de uma cidade negligenciada poderia ser lida como uma heterotopia que é altamente controlada por guardas e câmeras de segurança. Tal organização segue o slogan comercial do empreendimento Ilha do Sul: "Uma infraestrutura voltada ao lazer, conforto e segurança." Este slogan engloba tudo aquilo que São Paulo não é.

O esquema do Condomínio *Ilha Sul* tornou-se um paradigma para o desenvolvimento imobiliário para a classe média no século 21 como também um símbolo do fracasso do desenvolvimento público voltados à cultura, ao esporte e ao lazer, como parques e praças públicas. Mas em termos de propaganda e preferências dos usuários, todavia, os novos empreendimentos ficaram ainda mais sofisticados hoje em dia. Tanto inspirados pelas tipologias de châteaux Franceses ou de villas Espanholhas, a arquitetura destes empreendimentos é raramente concebida com a participação de famosos arquitetos de São Paulo, como é o caso do arquiteto paulista vencedor do Pritzker Prize em 2006, Paulo Mendes da Rocha e seus discípulos, membros da chamada Escola Paulista ou Brutalismo Paulista. Se as elites abraçaram a arquitetura moderna brasileira nos anos cinquenta, este não tem sido o caso nas últimas décadas. Tal recusa deu-se, sobretudo como uma decorrência da ausência de nomes como o do arquiteto João Batista Vilanova Artigas (1915-85), considerado o "fundador" da Escola Paulista e de outros de seus representantes, exilados durante a ditadura militar no Brasil (1964-85.)

Como resultado, os arquitetos paulistas tiveram que começar a questionar a efetiva extensão do seu campo de ação explorando estratégias alternativas para entender o território e conseguir atuar no ambiente construído. Se por um lado a incorporadora vem intensificando o isolamento dos novos condomínios fechados, alguns arquitetos deslocaram seu foco de interesse, voltando-se, sobretudo a trabalhos de
p.038 infraestrutura. Tais arquitetos enfatizam o valor público e o caráter sistêmico do projeto de infraestrutura, visando principalmente através dos mesmos à costura de fragmentos urbanos.

Como programas públicos dedicados à transformação da educação, habitação, higiene, inundações, e gestão de recursos hídricos estão sendo implementados em São Paulo, estes arquitetos acreditam na necessidade de urbanizar e expandir os valores de trais projetos de infraestrutura em curso. Estas intervenções destinam-se a maximizar investimentos públicos e engendrar urbanidade *à tout prix*. Os *Centros de Educação Unificada* (CEU) construídos pela Prefeitura de São Paulo entre 2002 e 2004, são um exemplo. Cada CEU consiste em um grupo de instalações de esporte, cultura, e educação espacialmente distribuídos em três edifícios pré-fabricados, articulados por uma praça. Para Alexandre Delijaicov, um dos arquitetos responsáveis pelo projeto, a sigla "CEU" —adotado pelo prefeito de São Paulo à época—deveria em realidade ser traduzido como *Centros de Estruturação Urbana.* Como Renato Anelli colocou, "s CEU querem inaugurar uma nova urbanidade para seus bairros. Mas não se trata de fazer uma "tabula rasa" do local. Esses partidos não se limitam a uma ação no campo do objeto e buscam identificar e transformar a situação territorial da área onde eles se instalam." Por isso, o plano era construir uma rede de CEUs em três fases: vinte e um na primeira, outros vinte e quatro na segunda, e para organizar um CEU especial, re-articular quarenta e cinco instalações municipais na terceira fase.

Ainda que o projeto tenha sido interrompido por razões de ordem política, a extensão das intervenções podem ser demonstradas em números. De fato na primeira fase, vinte e um CEUs foram construídos, com quatorze instalações cada, totalizando 294 novas instalações públicas localizadas na periferia da RMSP. As instalações de teatro e esportes dos CÉUS devem também servir as escolas públicas de ensino médio e fundamental nos seus arredores. Mas o CÉU pretende estruturar não somente as instalações ao seu redor, como também a cidade em si: em cada local onde o CEU foi implantado, os arquitetos envolvidos tentaram desenhar as ruas ao redor, muitas vezes não pavimentadas, providenciando novos equipamentos urbanos—como bancos, postes de luz, e pontes sobre riachos—e organizando ambos paisagismo e orla fluvial. Contrário às premissas preconizadas por Prestes Maia e adotadas em São Paulo, Delijaicov é um forte defensor da utilização das orlas fluviais da RMSP, com outras finalidades para além da função viáriae da navegação de seus rios e córregos. Assim o CEU foi utilizado como um parâmetro para intervenção em escala metropolitana com o objetivo de oferecer educação, infraestrutura, urbanização e urbanidade para as regiões mais pobres da RMSP. Os projetos urbanos do escritório de arquitetura MMBB, tais quais "Watery Voids" e "Antonico Creek" são dois outros exemplos de intervenções do mesmo tipo.

Para combater os problemas de drenagem e frequentes alagamentos, o Estado de São Paulo construiu os chamados *piscinões*, que podem ser descritos como grandes bacias que coletam o excesso de água. Dos cento e trinta e um *piscinões* planejados para abrigar 15.5 milhões e metros cúbicos de água, somente quarenta e dois foram construídos. Durante grande parte do ano, tais bacias são não mais do que imensos buracos situados no meio da cidade. MMBB Arquitetos, um escritório de arquitetura baseado

em São Paulo atualmente formado pelos arquitetos Fernando de Mello Franco, Marta Moreira e Milton Braga, formulou a hipótese de que a emergência de uma nova classe social na RMSP poderia oferecer a oportunidade de investigação de novas demandas para a urbanização da cidade. Com o projeto "Vazios de Água" MMBB clama pelo abandono da visão exclusivamente técnica dos trabalhos de
p.040 infraestrutura referentes a tais piscinões, e pela participação efetiva na transformação das periferias de São Paulo. Assim, os arquitetos propuseram a reprogramação deste sistema hidrográfico através da formação de uma nova rede de espaços públicos que buscam fortalecer laços sociais, criando ao mesmo tempo um sistema estruturante na periferia. Na maior parte do ano, tais bacias podem servir de playground, campos de futebol, parques para skate ou pontos de encontro. Tal como os mapas psicogeográficos de Debord, o diagrama desenhado pelo MMBB para "Vazios de Água" apresenta uma arquitetura interessada não somente nos fragmentos programados, como também nas redes de conexão que poderiam ser estabelecidas entre estes vazios urbanos.

Outro exemplo de atuação seguindo a mesma linha é o projeto urbano "Córrego do Antonico" (2008) também desenvolvido pelo MMBB Arquitetos que é, por sua vez, parte do programa de urbanização de favelas implementado pela Secretaria Municipal de Habitação de São Paulo. A intervenção situa-se em Paraisópolis, a segunda maior favela da cidade que se formou justamente pelo fracasso de um antigo projeto urbano. A área de intervenção encerra um quilômetro quadrado, ou 0.386 milhas quadradas, composta por uma população de aproximadamente sessenta mil habitantes. O córrego atravessa uma malha ortogonal que foi irresponsavelmente construída em uma topografia que é altamente irregular. O projeto consiste na elaboração de um novo sistema de drenagem e na reconfiguração de espaços abertos ao longo do córrego, que tal como os piscinões de "Vazios de Água," foi também reprogramado. Nas palavras do arquiteto Fernando de Mello Franco, "O projeto irá criar uma espinha dorsal compreendendo uma sequência de espaços públicos, similar a uma das mais poderosas estruturas espaciais em cidades brasileiras: o calçadão—ou seja, um corredor pavimentado que é muitas vezes utilizado para fazer a transição entre a praia e o tecido urbano".

Para MMBB, a presença de um corpo de água reprogramado poderia se configurar como uma das principais estruturas locais que, no contexto de Paraisópolis, seria capaz de promover não somente a construção do domínio público no imaginário de seus habitantes, como também uma associação dos espaços livres aos usos que a cultura da praia urbana pode evocar. MMBB define esta cultura de praia como "uso espontâneo do espaço que permite culturalmente uma ativa e desejável co-existência, porém não totalmente desprovida de conflitos."

Para uma melhor compreensão da razão pela qual os arquitetos paulistas como MMBB, Delijaicov e Mendes Rocha se interessam pelo tema da água, dos rios, praias e embarcações urbanos poderíamos recorrer à explicação de Michel Foucault sobre o porquê de o navio ter sido historicamente não apenas o maior instrumento de desenvolvimento econômico, mas também a maior reserva de imaginação. "O navio é a heterotopia por excelência. Nas civilizações sem embarcações, os sonhos secam, a espionagem substitui a aventura, e a polícia toma o lugar dos piratas."

Irão os arquitetos e usuários na RMSP seram capazes de depender menos na policia e guardas de segurança e mais em navio? Capazes ou não, estes projetos indicam um possível campo de investigação. Certamente a troca de desafios de infraestrutura e incorporação residencial em uma florescente metropole como a RMSP poderia servir como uma apropriada inspiração para uma nova busca de mapeamento mental e assim programação no nível de um studio de arquitetura.

p.042 III. INTERSECÇÕES URBANAS: TRABALHO DE ESTÚDIO NA YALE

p.044 BEM VINDO A SÃO PAULO

Com o crescimento da população e dos fluxos migratórios nacionais e internacionais, São Paulo tem crescido rapidamente nos últimos 100 anos a uma densidade de 9.000 pessoas por quilômetro quadrado e uma população de mais de 17 milhões de pessoas. É uma densa megalópole global em que as camadas de experimentos urbanos, desenvolvimento e construção relacionados aos automóveis resultaram em uma cidade vibrante, multicêntrica e caracterizada por sua disjunção. São Paulo é uma "cidade de muros", segundo a antropóloga Teresa Caldeira, ainda que os processos de distanciamento social e enclaustro tenham coincidido com a democratização política, com o crescimento dos movimentos sociais, e com múltiplos esforços para reconhecer e estabelecer serviços para os espaços informais da cidade.

Enquanto a atenção da crítica é voltada à forma como as áreas pobres de São Paulo se relacionam com as áreas extremamente ricas, o Estúdio será focado em moradia para a emergente classe média da cidade. Entre 2004 e 2008, a percentagem de pessoas de classe média no Brasil aumentou dez por cento. Combinado com programas sociais como o "Bolsa Família" para combater tanto a pobreza extrema como a desigualdade social, e o aumento de 100% do salário mínimo na última década, o aumento recente da classe média tem profundas implicações para os espaços urbanos da cidade em relação ao consumo e à moradia, tanto formais como informais. O IBGE estima que há um déficit de cerca de oito milhões de moradias no Brasil, que vão desde a habitação de baixa renda até a de renda alta.

Um novo projeto para a classe média com uso misto em uma área de 181.000 metros quadrados, adjacente à Marginal Tietê e a Rodovia Rio Tietê em São Paulo. O projeto é complexo, tanto em sua disposição periférica para o centro urbano quanto para os requisitos de desempenho definidos pelo empreendedor, Tishman Speyer. O zoneamento permite 325.000 metros quadrados de construção residencial, varejo e comercial. O acesso ao local, linhas elétricas de alta potencia na superfície e inúmeros existentes e deteriorados prédios históricos fornecem um plano ainda mais complexo de empreendimento, assim como o necessário o desenvolvimento das fases do projeto.

Os alunos foram solicitados a abordar o projeto do ponto de vista de ambas as designers e empreendedores, e envolver questões de agenda, de risco, de flexibilidade, valor, taxas de retorno, escala, clareza formal, articulação do complexo, sensibilidade ambiental e climática, uso de cor e textura e da relação do edifício com o paisagismo. Perguntamos: Quais são as possibilidades para a criação de um novo espaço urbano que seja seguro e acessível? Como o projeto distribuirá os requisitos de densidade e estacionamento que foram primeiramente assumidos pelo empreendedor do pro-forma em uma área cujo contexto imediato foi de muito menor densidade? Os projetos resultantes investigaram novas abordagens para o espaço público partilhado e de acesso dentro de um empreendimento privado. Eles integram as práticas sustentáveis de ventilação natural, sombreamento e da redução das inundações sazonais, considerando ao mesmo tempo criatividade nas formas arquitetônicas para habitação densa e programas de uso misto, e descobrindo maneiras de conectar um local isolado com o resto da cidade.

p.060 DO CENTRO À PERIFERIA: BANDEIRANTES, SÃO PAULO

p.061 Localizado a seis milhas fora da cidade central, o local do projeto do estúdio, Bandeirantes, é isolado da cidade ao seu redor por claros limites físicos, mas ele fica em um cruzamento de diversos usos urbanos e formas. Ele é cercado por um loteamento de classe média-altas na parte oeste, um parque da cidade ao norte, um loteamento de classe trabalhadora para o leste, e a auto-estrada, rio, e loteamentos industriais ao sul e sudoeste. Acima da linha terrestre fios de eletrecidade passam ao longo da borda leste separando a parte superior da inferior do local.

Funcionando originalmente como uma fazenda, o local tornou-se um matadouro no início do século vinte até 1960, quando foi vendida e abandonada por 50 anos. Há uma série de fábricas abandonadas na parte superior da propriedade, incluindo uma estrutura de marco histórico que antigamente funcionava como um clube para funcionários.

São Domingo, o prédio baixo ao redor, bairro residencial de classe média, tem uma população de aproximadamente 168.000 habitantes e é marcantemente menos denso do que ambas as areas adjacentes e a densidade necessária nos estudos iniciais do empreendedor.A proforma inicial precisava de 2.500 unidades residenciais e programas de apoio para sustentar a nova comunidade. O empreendedor, Tishman Speyer, explorou vários cenários, incluindo escritórios, residências, e espaços comerciais. No cenário mais drástico, a porção inferior do site seria vendidos a um operador comercial para tornar'se um shopping center.

Em uma cidade marcada pela extrema densidade, terreno subdesenvolvido, isolamento e a baixa densidade dos bairros adjacentes, esta apresentou um desafio único no desenvolvimento da periferia do local. O projeto ofereceu uma oportunidade de analisar como novas abordagens ao design urbano podem oferecer alternativas para as repetitivas torres que pontilham o horizonte, incorporar a sustentabilidade como um princípio organizador, e apresentam diferentes graus de acesso e segurança a estas cidades, espaços públicos, e a porta da frente de uma casa.

p.072 PROJETOS

p.073 **Resumo do Studio** O estúdio começou com um curso intensivo sobre conceitos de mercado imobiliário e o desenvolvimento em São Paulo, com Nate Shanok da Tishman Speyer. Ele forneceu uma visão geral das ferramentas utilizadas pela Tishman Speyer para analisar os mercados residenciais e comerciais, incluindo uma extensiva pesquisa de mercado e modelos de cenários de desenvolvimento. Ele também reviu um número de cenários para o terreno do projeto, oferecendo aos alunos um entendimento do impacto de diferentes tamanhos de unidades, misturas residenciais, programas de comércio e varejo, subdivisões, fases, e um entendimento de infraestrutura no envelope zoneado.

Na primeira tarefa, os estudantes participaram em uma conversação presentemente acontecendo entre planejadores, empreendedores, designers, funcionários, ativistas e residentes de São Paulo sobre o conceito e direção para a os espaços urbanos da cidade e arquitetura. Os estudantes perguntaram o que eles precisariam para entender a cidade, sua história e sua política; como responder aos problemas de segurança; quais são as camadas das classes sociais da cidade, e quais são os espaços e a forma da cidade? Logo após, em grupo de dois, eles apresentaram estas questões urbanas, falando sobre infraestrutura, demografia, clima, práticas construtivas, e produção econômica e cultural.

Eles também conduziram uma pesquisa dos projetos da metade do século vinte dos arquitetos brasileiros Oscar Niemeyer, Lina Bo Bardi, Paulo Mendes da Rocha e João Vilanova Artigas, assim como do paisagista Roberto Burle Marx. Particularmente, os estudantes foram instruídos para considerar o uso de formas e massas, cor e material, técnicas de fachadas, implantação e estratégias de paisagismo pelo arquiteto, todos ensinaram aos alunos a escala de desenhos e estudos analíticos de predecessores residenciais.

Na próxima etapa, usando um conjunto de critérios para analisar seus desenhos, os alunos rapidamente desenvolveram três cenários enfatizando suas aproximações e estratégia para uma implantação, representando a planta com um desenho aéreo ou com maquetes e perspectivas. Após, eles prepararam um plano piloto inicial.

Na viagem de uma semana ao Brasil, eles apresentaram seus conceitos ao time de empreendimento e encontraram arquitetos, planejadores, e acadêmicos trabalhando em São Paulo. Eles visitaram incorporações feitas pela Tishman Speyer e visitaram prédios em São Paulo, Brasília e Rio de Janeiro para ver o trabalho dos arquitetos brasileiros que haviam estudado.

Após a metade do semestre, os alunos mudaram o foco da escala do plano piloto para o projeto do terreno específico, que compromete edifícios residenciais individualmente e seus espaços abertos arredor. Na segunda metade do semestre, cada aluno desenvolveu seus desenhos em varias escalas, com ênfase particularmente na integração e implementação de espaços públicos e semiprivados. O trabalho respondeu ao grau de fechamento e da articulação das superfícies exteriores horizontais e verticais: fachadas dos edifícios, paisagismo, e os espaços de transição entre a cidade e o interior.

p.074
DISTRITO BANDEIRANTES DE ARTE
Rebecca Garnett

O Distrito Bandeirantes de Arte propõe um modelo não convencional de empreendimento para capitalizar as restrições do terreno, criando um novo recinto artístico, posicionando assim a próspera cultura artística do Brasil no coração do empreendimento. Tendo sido uma vez utilizada como matadouro, a estrutura parecida com ruínas iluminadas no céu ao centro do caro terreno hoje é reformulada como um centro comunitário e das artes similar ao SESC Pompéia—um bem sucedido empreendimento de artes e recreação em São Paulo, famoso pela arquitetura de Lina Bo Bardi. Os espaços industriais longos são idéias para configurações flexíveis de exposições de arte e atuam como um motor cultural e econômico para este empreendimento perifericamente localizado. Ao redor desta praça pública de artes, uma malha solta de um tecido "caminhavel" e de múltiplas escalas quebram o empreendimento de 2.200 unidades residenciais em bairros menores. Três escalas de habitação são desenvolvidas de acordo com a variada topografia e as condições paisagísticas onde elas estão localizadas: cada escala é então espetada por uma coluna cultural compreendendo espaços varejistas, habitações para artistas e instalações comunitárias de recreação.

Trezentas e noventa unidades de casas geminadas mediaram doze metros de desnível natural na borda ao sul, aproveitando as vistas através dos rios em direção ao perfil da cidade. Embora parecendo estarem situadas em um programa denso, cada unidade tem espaço ao ar livre e quatro exposições que proporcionam sombreamento e ventilação nos meses do verão úmido. No meio do terreno, 600 unidades de habitações médias são definidas em um platô e fornecem uma conexão física com os bairros residenciais adjacentes. Relembrando as chamadas superquadras de Brasília, os prédios nestes blocos semi-privados são erguidos acima do solo para criar uma sensação de transparência e conectividade ao nível do solo. Acessíveis aos moradores do bairro, amenidades comuns ocorrem logo abaixo e acima do platô; jardins submersos e instalações de recreação ocorrem no nível mais baixo, e plataformas de coleta são erguidas acima. Edifícios médios projetam sombra no chão e asseguram ventilação máxima para as unidades acima; fachadas são equipadas com telas apropriadamente orientadas para mitigar ângulos de sol forte, permitindo uma ventilação adequada. Finalmente, arranha-céus com bases pequenas e estruturas de colunas são posicionados no auto, encostas arborizadas ao norte, posicionados para tirar vantagem dos pontos de vista amplos e caros de São Paulo. Como o bairro mediano, estas unidades acomodam-se às torres adjacentes existentes e compartilham o acesso conveniente do parque no extremo norte.

Esta proposta traz à questão o uso dominante e onipresente da tipologia torre arranha-céu complementando o modelo vertical com outros tipos adequados regionalmente. Desta forma, uma variedade de estilos de vida urbanos é fornecida aos moradores de classe média de São Paulo mesmo estes estando longe do centro da cidade.

p.082 JARDIM BRASILEIRO Lis Cena

O projeto esta dividido em três partes: duas residenciais e uma comercial. As torres residenciais estão agrupadas juntas para criar duas comunidades distintas; uma no meio e outra nas partes superiores do terreno. Uma paisagem colorida, de variadas camadas, de pequenas piscinas, plantas nativas e campos de atletismo oferecem conexões ativas entre as torres altas e as instalações compartilhadas. Elementos tradicionais de jardim criam superfícies rígidas e macias que se costuram juntas para definir áreas públicas e privadas. Na parte mais abaixo do terreno, um grande complexo varejista se estende até a cidade e é posicionado para tornar-se um destino de compras.

Em resposta aos contextos culturais e ambientais da bela paisagem urbana e do patrimônio arquitetônico moderno de São Paulo, Jardim Brasileiro endereça três tipos de programas: social urbano, ecológico, ambiental e de tecnologia. Cada aspecto programático do projeto arquitetônico manifesta uma distinta estratégia que se elabora na poderosa e expressiva linguagem da arquitetura Moderna Brasileira.

A primeira estratégia negocia a difícil questão de segurança pessoal, que aparece como um grande espectro de problema social e de arquitetura para a cultura urbana do Brasil. Ao invés de delinear limites espaciais explícitos, cercas altas e portões, o projeto está preocupado com a idéia de fazer um local—um ambiente de distinta vista e experiências formais e uma série de limites planejados em camadas. A segunda estratégia tem como foco o uso do vento para ventilação natural. Esta tentativa de ajudar o resfriamento e a aeração dos espaços ao ar livre e dos espaços interiores das habitações é fundamental para o desenho da implantação e das torres; cada configuração dos edifícios responde aos ventos predominantes. Finalmente, a estratégia arquitetônica das fachadas responde ao crítico problema de exposição solar durante longos períodos de extremo calor em São Paulo: uma clara, mas complexa estrutura de cortinas em camadas e painéis emoldurados de sombreamento por suas diversas espessuras são utilizadas para visualmente animar a experiência dos pedestres nos jardins na base das torres. A profunda articulação das fachadas leste e oeste criam uma textura vertical que está respondendo ao clima e aos componentes de paisagismo abaixo.

p.090 CIDADE VIZINHANÇA Catherine Anderson

Os moradores da Cidade Vizinhança aspiram viver em um bairro de densidade média com habitações baixas, própria escala e identidade e com calçadas cheias de atividades. Todavia, esta visão e uma meta desafiadora de alcançar porque a eficiência dos custos de densidade e da verdadeira necessidade pela segurança tem feito um bairro urbano de sucesso para a classe média inviável. Cidade Vizinhança tenta capturar as características fundamentais desta densidade enquanto respondendo a escala, identidade e espaços públicos em São Paulo.

Na escala urbana, o plano piloto organiza o programa de varejo ao redor de uma rua urbana e de espaços públicos, incluindo uma faixa para pedestres. Para alcançar isto, a incorporadora faz parceria com empreendedores especializados em varejo para criar uma imagem urbana mais rica, ao invés de um Shopping Center fechado. Os espaços públicos das principais ruas e passagens são separados da zona residencial privada por um deslocamento transversal, assegurando privacidade e segurança sem recorrer às existentes barreiras rígidas que mantém os residentes de toda São Paulo isolados. Além disso, a zona elevada residencial é adjacente a rua pública, permitindo aos moradores acesso visual para a vida pública, mas não compromissando a sua segurança.

Na escala comunitária, o terreno é dividido em múltiplas zonas para variar escalas, densidade, e a comercialização. Para alcançar um retorno mínimo de investimento, o empreendimento deve abrigar 2.380 unidades habitacionais. Utilizando a configuração de torre proposta, esta meta se traduz em 17 torres no terreno de 180.000 metros quadrados. Ao invés de distribuir as torres igualmente, o plano piloto agrupa de três até cinco torres em densos e únicos agrupamentos que possibilitam maiores extensões de áreas abertas. O espaço construído e o paisagismo se alternam em oito estrias através do terreno, variando em escala e caráter para oferecer identidade e diferenciação, uma proposta natural de fases.

Na escala dos edifícios, cada torre dentro da Cidade Vizinhança é dividida conceitualmente desde um prédio de 28 andares até sete prédios médios de quatro andares empilhados em cima um do outro. Este desenho é alcançado com o esculpimento de espaços públicos em incrementos de quatro andares ao longo da altura das torres para oferecer instalações públicas de menor escala. As vinte unidades habitacionais podem acessar cada instalação—por exemplo, parques, jardins, instalações de recreação, e espaços internos de encontro—exclusivamente, permitindo um senso de comunidade de escala menor dentro da torre e aliviando a densidade.

O programa vertical de espaços públicos e instalações é mais do que um elemento programático; isto ativa a fachada e define a imagem do edifício—e, por extensão, o empreendimento—para operar como uma ferramenta de marketing para a escala única e estrutura espacial do Cidade Vizinhança. Nas escalas urbanas, comunitárias e prediais, o senso de identidade e local começam a crescer gradualmente com os ocupantes se mudando de um empreendimento com 8.500 pessoas para um aglomerado de 1.960 e para um edifício de 490 pessoas até a uma comunidade de setenta pessoas.

p.096 **JARDIM VIVENTE Hilary Zaic**

Este projeto aproveita a exuberante natureza do terreno existente criando um novo parque semi-público rodeado por uma série de casas geminadas e torres residenciais. Ligados formal e fisicamente a um parque na parte norte do terreno, bem como ao novo complexo de varejo na parte sul, o novo parque seria inicialmente acessível apenas a moradores do Jardim Vivente, mas tudo será aberto ao público de fora.

Os prédios e a topografia trabalham juntos para oferecer pontos de controle na entrada e uma sensação de proteção que elimina a necessidade de paredes de proteção e portões de entrada. Ao longo do terreno, o parque se transforma em campos de recreação, atrações com água e um denso bosque de árvores. A circulação de automóveis permanece no lado de fora do parque, estabelecendo nódulos de entrada onde os moradores podem entrar no estacionamento no subsolo que está eficientemente abaixo do projetado paisagismo Dentro destes nódulos, instalações públicas se estendem dentro do paisagismo central para formar bolsas de espaços compartilhados em diversos graus de privacidade em planta e em corte.

Tipologias residenciais altas e baixas coexistem para oferecer uma variedade de tipologias de moradias. As casas geminadas em cima do estacionamento e outros espaços trazem o parque até os prédios, maximizando os espaços ao ar livre. Um passeio semiprivado conecta o parque com as casas mais baixas, hall de entrada dos prédios altos, espaços de descanso e programas públicos. As fases de construção representam uma importante parte na evolução do parque. Começando na parte de traz do terreno e indo em frente, cada fase é equipada com uma estrutura de garagens no subterrâneo e seus espaços para infraestrutura requeridos. O parque se torna a identidade do projeto inteiro, apagando limites do terreno com a paisagem ao redor e permitindo até mesmo as torres ecoarem a fauna local através do desenho de sua proteção solar.

p.104 **COBERTURA DO SOLO: SÃO PAULO Anja Turowski**

Desafiando a noção do tradicional desenvolvimento torre-no-parque, este projecto procura envolver o plano de apoio de uma forma que reapropria o espaço geralmente não reclamado e muitas vezes negligenciado entre arranha-céus. Para ativar este espaço, o esquema elabora torres residenciais simplificadas no terreno complementadas por densas habitações geminadas. A agregação de unidades habitacionais de médio porte resultam em um parque paisagístico que desce pelo meio do terreno, seguindo a topografia natural. Uma sinuosa estrada de acesso tece através do terreno conectando o parque e casas geminadas.

As unidades habitacionais geminadas oferecem espaços verdes ao ar livre para cada unidade, enquanto que a orientação e inclinação para o interior do terreno fornecem uma paisagem variada ao novo parque. As unidades são padronizadas, mas, seguindo a inclinação natural do local, a forma e a composição fluida oferecem uma bela vista para a paisagem. Ao contrário de tipologias geminadas tradicionais que usam a topografia existente para agrupar casas com densidade média, esta estrategia lamina as unidades habitacionais no topo do existente plano de solo para criar um ventre artificial entre a estrutura residencial e o solo. A parte inferior das unidades separadas abrigam instalações de espaços comunais, como creches, lojas e instalações recreativas, oferecendo estacionamento para residentes de ambos as torres e das casas geminadas.

Em contraste com a borda rarefeita e o desnível no interior do tereno, as fachadas das casa na rua se conectam firmamente à estrada para criar um ambiente denso e urbano. As fachadas são articuladas de tal forma para proporcionar janelas voltadas para o interior do complexo, distinguindo-se os elementos de maior escala do programa comunitário, como os espaços de performance, desde os menores, bem como as lojas. Esta estratégia permite que programas públicos e privados possam ser orientados para lados opostos, proporcionando privacidade para as unidades habitacionais e oferecendo o acesso público a todas as comodidades comuns.

Os vários componentes de construção deste projeto são montados e integrados com várias estruturas compostas que podem ser feitas em quatro fases. Os próprios edifícios são compostos de grandes vãos de concreto, que são estruturados de acordo com as exigências do estacionamento abaixo e ajustados para as unidades de pequena escala padronizada acima. Todas as unidades residenciais podem ser acessadas diretamente a partir das áreas de estacionamento através de corredores que são iluminados por cima por penetrações nos andares de habitações geminadas e através de portas de entradas frontais comunais que são localizadas nas ruas de fachada.

p.112

BARRIO REAL **Steve Ybarra**

As complexidades de Bandeirantes, São Paulo, se estende além de implantação, programa, e densidade. Mais do que somente um desenvolvimento residencial, Bandeirantes é um bairro em sua infância. "Bairro real" sugere um primeiro passo para a criação de um senso de identidade para a nova e exponencial crescente demográfica, a classe media brasileira. A forma do desenvolvimento urbano é inspirada—não em escala, mas em inspiração—pelos bairros Jardins em São Paulo nos quais o alastramento de desenvolvimento de alto padrão em São Paulo é contido na bacia, permitindo uma vibrante, caminhavel e modesto distrito ganhar forma em seu centro.

O componente residencial do projeto compreende duas áreas: Um grupo de seis torres localizado no ponto mais ao norte, numa parte bastante arborizada do projeto, e uma linha de seis prédios mediando a borda do platô na porção sul do projeto, separando a porção residencial do projeto do desenvolvimento comercial abaixo. Dentre estes dois densamente habitados grupos esta uma serie de modestas casas geminadas, criando uma malha de prazerosas, caminhaveis ruas que beneficiam o bairro. A Rua Principal do bairro, constituindo-se de funções, comerciais, educacionais e publicas, conecta estas três áreas do projeto entre si e com a existente malha residencial no oeste.

Ao lado da Rua Principal ocorrera um parque público linear que será espelhado no desenvolvimento na borda mais ao leste por outro parque linear que primeiramente servira os residentes do bairro. Instalações para esportes ao ar livre serão localizadas aqui, e o espaço aberto conectara os caminhos verdes no centro de cada condomínio entre si e com o existente parque público localizado no ponto mais ao norte do projeto.

O Bairro Real incorporará práticas sustentáveis em diferentes escalas. Todas as unidades residenciais do projeto terão ventilação natural, enquanto que as grandes áreas verdes dos espaços abertos ajudaram no gerenciamento de águas pluviais e prevenção de alagamentos. A densidade atingida com as torres agrupadas permitirá um mais eficiente transporte público, servindo ambos os ônibus e futuras paradas de metro. Mais importante, a coerência, com as mesmas dimensões os blocos permitiram o crescimento sustentável através do tempo; cada parcela tem a habilidade de mudar e crescer sem que afete o caráter geral da pública esfera do bairro. Neste sentido, o Bairro Real atua como um modelo para o crescimento futuro e desenvolvimento de São Paulo e fornece espaços públicos e residenciais sustentáveis e vibrantes integrados com seus arredores.

p.118

BANDEIRANTES: VEJA PRIMEIRO **Carmel Greer**

O projeto procura a topografia natural do terreno e a exuberante paisagem para criar um projeto caracterizado significantemente pela sua densidade e proximidade com a natureza. Uma série de plintos se estende dentro da floresta e navega o terreno do projeto, permitindo a exuberância, áreas íngremes permanecer imperturbável enquanto que aproveitando os belos pontos de vistas para São Paulo. Os plintos acomodam espelhos d'agua, elementos de paisagismo, e outras instalaçōs como estacionamento residencial localizado abaixo, conectando um discreto e conveniente estacionamento com a circulação vertical de cada edifício. A superfície de cada plinto é aproximadamente meio andar acima do solo, minimizando excavação e rachaduras. A estratégia reduz custos iniciais de construção enquanto providencia elementos de segurança e estacionamento que são críticos para uma incorporação de sucesso na área de comércio residencial.

Torres alinham a borda mais oeste do terreno, culminando em uma monumental torre residencial que serve como um mecanismo de propaganda para Tishman Speyer. A mais alta torre do esquema é visível pela rodovia, pelo rio, e pela área central de São

Paulo, distinguido o terreno do Tishman Speyer dos outros projetos residenciais. Cada unidade dentro das torres residenciais abaixo tem uma sacada personalizável forrada com a rica madeira brasileira. A madeira é também usada em venezianas, oferecendo sombra em cada janela. Estes elementos oferecem riqueza de materiais e um sistema de controle passivo da luz solar para a torre, um tipo de construção muitas vezes caracterizada por esterilidade. A sacada e as instalações de cozinha ao ar livre são personalizadas pelo dono da unidade, oferecendo diferenciação entre as unidades que são visíveis pelo lado de fora.

Um centro comercial ocupa o ponto mais abaixo do terreno. Um caminho sinuoso costura entre as torres e a paisagem, oferecendo a experiência de uma rápida estrada na encosta em um ambiente de urbano de trafego congestionado. Uma espinha central de calcadas e jardins conectam cada plinto com o nódulo central e permite os pedestres navegar através do projeto e dentro de parques adjacentes e áreas residenciais.

p.124 UM MODELO DE TRABALHO PARA IDENTIDADE **Alejandro Fernandez de Mesa**

Uma das mais notáveis características do desenho brasileiro é seu sucesso em criar espaços públicos provocativos. Como parte do diálogo entre o arquiteto e o incorporador, o espaço público com sucesso não pode somente fortalecer o senso de comunidade, mas também pode atuar como estratégia de marca para a incorporação. Um loteamento privado residencial de 41, 500 unidades no Brasil não pode, todavia, sucessivamente existir como uma coleção de unidades individuais sem uma malha conectiva, o que é o espaço público definido. O objetivo deste projeto é oferecer um modelo de trabalho no qual uma clara hierarquia de espaços públicos pode ser atingida. Além disso, este modelo de trabalho conta com as instalações que são características de tais incorporações bem como as exigências de desempenho do empreendedor.

Nesta proposta, os prédios são organizados em grupos de baixas torres como uma crítica direta ao arranjamento modernista de Brasília e seus super-blocos. Nesta tradição modernista, os prédios são implantados no terreno em uma maneira racional que responde as preocupações ambientais e oferecem generosos espaços públicos. No entanto, o que a idéia Modernista falha em oferecer neste terreno em particular é um senso de controle e a habilidade de manter estes espaços públicos em uma maneira de conectar a arquitetura e seus habitantes.

Este projeto fornece às três escalas de espaços públicos. A primeira, chamada "agrupamento", explora as relações entre os dois prédios: o de tamanho médio e a torre. Aqui, um paisagismo em dois níveis conecta os dois edifícios para oferecer sombreamento para cada prédio e conexão visual a partir do espaço de utilidade para o domínio privado no interior dos aglomerados. A segunda escala, o bloco, conecta os mais íntimos espaços de cada aglomerado e demarca a circulação por todo o terreno; a escala do bloco também funciona como uma forma eficiente de construção de seqüência. Finalmente, a maior escala do projeto é um vazio central, ou a praça, que é conectada com parte da rede de aglomerados e espaços públicos de médio porte que juntos definem a comunidade. O resultado geral é uma série de experiências sensitivas que são instigados por uma escala reconhecível e materialidade. O projeto é organizado em torno destas mudanças de escala no paisagismo e desenvolvimento em fases.

p.132 A PRAÇA EM BANDEIRANTES **Bradley Baer**

A Praça em Bandeirantes redefine densidade habitacional em uma das mais rápidas populações em crescimento do mundo, ao mesmo tempo endereçando questões de segurança, espaços públicos e senso de comunidade. Para alcançar isto, o plano piloto propõe uma série de prédios residenciais de meio nível que se afunilam da praça central, o foco principal do projeto. Esta praça central contém um campo de futebol tamanho oficial, centro comunitário e espaço varejista. Esta estratégica configuração de unidades residenciais e espaços públicos oferecem um senso de comunidade e segurança enquanto evita a necessidade de um tradicional muro de proteção. Enquanto que torres criam passagens para vento e projetam longas sombras, uma série de pequenos prédios de meio nível faz referência pra a rica história brasileira de construções baixas de habitação e permite a penetração de luz solar dentro das unidades e espaços públicos.

Os requerimentos do programa residencial são alcançados e excedidos por dez prédios de 10-12 andares com capacidade potencial para mais de 2.800 unidades que mantém uma escala íntima em comparação com as típicas torres de luxo. Os espaços resultantes entre os arredores e as casas formam uma série de bairros temáticos que oferecem uma variedade de instalações, estilo de vida e escala. Uma rota sinuosa media a topografia acentuada do terreno e oferece a cada edifício uma área de embarque para automóveis. A configuração funicular dos layouts das residências oferece varias orientações para os apartamentos: algumas unidades de frente para a cidade, outras tendo vistas para a nova praça e campos, e algumas orientadas para as praças ao redor.

Uma série de vazios quebra a massa horizontal. O sol pode penetrar através das unidades e sacadas privadas. Estes cortes causam variações nos planos dos pisos, adicionando valor por diferenciar o layout dos apartamentos. De manhã, pouca luz ilumina a praça; no meio da tarde, treliças esculturais oferecem sombra do sol tropical.

Tendo como inspiração o pavimento "triângulo-quadrado-triângulo" nas ruas de São Paulo, cada fachada de cada prédio é composta de painéis modulares como versões escaladas do padrão do pavimento. Como um sistema modular customizado, os painéis sólidos podem também ser substituídos com venezianas inclinadas ou vidro para adaptarem-se as diferentes condições ambientais ou preferências pessoais.

p.142

MIRANTE Eliza Higgins

Mirante é uma proposta para 1.800 unidades que alcança o objetivo da incorporadora Pro Forma ao mesmo tempo endereçando percepções de segurança, comunidade, antecipando inundamentos sazonais e ecologia através de uma arquitetura que é contemporânea e brasileira.

Em português, mirante se traduz para "belvedere" ou "cidade vista".. Quatorze torres residenciais direcionam e definem uma paisagem escultural, criando uma série de planejados pátios enquanto mantendo uma forte conexão para o loteamento como um inteiro através de um espaço verde compartilhado, instalações sociais, e conexões visuais.

Durante as épocas de chuva em São Paulo—de novembro até abril—o jardim de dois níveis coleta e canaliza as águas pluviais para piscinas de retenção que se tornam campos de atletismo durante as épocas secas. Estas trocas metereológicas entre chuva e seca, e a mistura de instalações públicas e privadas oferecem um ativo paisagismo e uma comunidade social que podem ser experenciados tanto no solo quanto nos andares acima.

Cada torre manterá uma forte conexão com o solo através de paredes de concreto, que variam em profundidade para oferecer circulação vertical e suporte estrutural para as unidades residenciais em balanço acima. As torres em formato borboleta são estrategicamente arranjadas para capturar ventos prevalecentes para ventilação natural e maximizam as vistas para os pátios abaixo e para a cidade atrás. Para responder ao intenso sol brasileiro, venezianas de madeira finas feita de nativas e rapidamente renovável madeira pinus envolve as sacada de cada unidade criando uma fachada ativa. Painéis de tecidos coloridos nos trilhos internos oferecem um sombreamento adicional e animam a fachada com gradientes de cor de torre a torre. Esta mistura de cores mornas e materiais naturais ajudam a suavizar as torres e dissolvem a percepção da densidade do projeto.

Uma rua principal arterial comanda a circulação de veículos com a liberação de menores vias conectoras para fornecer acesso a cada torre. Separadamente da circulação principal, cada torre terá uma dedicada entrada e um deck de estacionamento, que será subterrâneo para preservar o paisagismo de pedestres acima. Instalações com acesso público—como academias, escolas, e varejo local—ocupam os vazios entre o parque público, pátios comunais e a topografia existente. Na base do terreno, um complexo de varejo e esportes abre-se para a estrada e a cidade atrás é escondido das residências em cima por um grande platô paisagístico que age como um término para o parque sinuoso que cobre o terreno.

p. 152

RESUMO DO DEBATE NO ESTÚDIO

p. 153

A seguir trechos das revises de Studio feitas ao longo do semester, organizados temáticamente.

O LEGADO DO MODERNISMO BRASILEIRO E SUSTENTABILIDADE

COMENTÁRIOS GERAIS

Claire Weisz Muitos de vocês assumiram o desafio de abordar o futuro do legado do Modernismo no Brasil, tanto em termos do ambiente e no aumento da demanda por habitação. Os projetos mais bem sucedidos foram aqueles que engajaram a seção como uma ferramenta para navegar a topografia e resolver adjacências programáticas. Minha sensação é que os projetos queriam alcançar um grau de economia, enquanto mantiveram um senso de lugar. Os esquemas seccionais efetuaram isto tanto na construção quanto no plano mestre.

Patrick Bellew Em termos da influência do Modernismo Brasileiro em muitas das propostas, é importante entender que embora estes possam ser edifícios modernistas bem sucedidos, na maioria dos casos eles não são bons ambientalmente-assim você deve empurrá-los para a frente 50 anos. Modernismo comemorou o novo sistema de ar condicionado, e o desafio para os engenheiros foi ver quanto resfriamento podia ser bombeado para dentro do prédio.

Agora sabemos que esta não é a solução correta e que isso deve ser feito de maneira diferente.

Quando olhamos a hierarquia de espaços em um projeto, tudo começa com o plano mestre. Como você orienta os edifícios e distribuir o programa? Uma vez estabelecida a organização geral, você deve olhar como abrir a arquitetura. Como você projeta a fenestração? Como organiza o plano para que a brisa percorra o edifício? Você deve pensar na escala do edifício, bem como na escala do apartamento. O arquiteto Australiano Glenn Murcutt na verdade senta-se dentro em cada ambiente afim de descobrir onde quais peças são mais confortáveis em momentos diferentes do dia. Você tem que multiplicar este exercício por 2.500. Se você errar, você terá 5.000 pessoas xingando o arquiteto assim como todos os alunos tem feito desde 1980 na sala de aula Modernista. A questão é como criar espaços habitáveis em um mundo com muito menos ar condicionado? Como arquitetos, vocês devem abraçar essas mudanças. Sustentabilidade e design andam lado a lado na criação de um projeto bem sucedido.

ESPAÇO PÚBLICO E COMUNIDADE
COMENTÁRIOS GERAIS

Peggy Deamer Podemos identificar pessoas jogando em parques, mas a sua noção de comunidade não pode apenas existir ao nível da concepção do parque. Como podemos apresentar-nos ao mundo real onde vamos às compras com o público em geral no mesmo local do loteamento residencial privado? Em certo momento, há um separador—no entanto as imagens fazem parecer que podemos estar dentro de um contexto maior e, a um certo ponto, sabemos que estamos separados do contexto.

p.154 **Cathleen McGuigan** A questão principal para mim é como lidar com a preocupação com a segurança para que o projeto não se torne uma ilha no São Paulo. O aspecto mais desafiador e interessante deste projeto é o que acontece no plano do solo através da definição e engajamento dos espaços públicos.

Peggy Deamer De que forma pode um projeto de controlar seu território enquanto mantém um senso de publicidade? Se você decidir abordar o site como um loteamento seguro privado, você tem que admitir que o projeto não é apenas uma ilha. Ele será visto por muitos, e este tem arestas, que devem interagir com o público. Como você pode ser um bom vizinho dessa maneira? Certamente, arquitetura de qualidade é uma das soluções. Este site é altamente visível em São Paulo, e há uma oportunidade de olhar para novos modelos sustentáveis de arquitetura e desenvolvimento que poderiam ser identificáveis de uma forma positiva para a cidade.

Audrey Matlock Eu gostaria de abordar três pontos: à variedade, a hierarquiae a segurança. A variedade de esquemas foi extraordinária e levou-nos a soluções muito criativas. Os projetos mais bem sucedidos estabeleceram uma hierarquia espacial, incluindo as relações entre o público e o privado, entre espaço aberto e com arestas borda, e entre tipologias de construção. Os projetos mais bem sucedidos foram baseadas em um entendimento das escalas múltiplas do espaço público. Finalmente, acho que a questão da segurança muito curiosa. Eu nunca fui a São Paulo, mas fui a lugares como o Cazaquistão, onde a segurança é uma grande preocupação. Não tenho certeza que é tanto uma questão de necessidade e de posse como tem sido destacado hoje. A noção de manter as pessoas fora é a antítese da comunidade, e como resolver essa contradição dentro do projeto é absolutamente fundamental. Você está criando um composto, ou você está criando uma parte integrante da cidade?

Andy Bow Qual é o DNA de São Paulo, e o que você pode aprender com ele? Você deve estabelecer uma hierarquia para promover um senso de comunidade e capturar o espírito do Brasil. Gostaria de pedir a todos para desenharem um axônio dos três primeiros níveis na base dos esquemas, porque são ambos o espaço público e os programas comunitários que fazem este projeto. Educação e cultura são extremamente importantes para um loteamento como este e dão vida à comunidade. Como estudantes, vocês devem empurrar e desafiar o programa a ser sustentável e ter uma visão avançada.

Tom Farrell Nós discutimos os requisitos do desenvolvimento de densidade e de estacionamento, mas um bom empreendedor percebe que grandes espaços públicos, senso de lugar, e paisagem, são essenciais para projetos de sucesso.

O LEGADO DO MODERNISMO BRASILEIRO
JARDIM BRASILEIRO POR LIS CENA

Audrey Matlock Este projeto faz um argumento muito convincente de como uma situação suburbana pode ser muito urbana. Você cria uma textura que é vertical ao invés de plana; as camadas de diferentes texturas de superfícies duras e macias e de espaços públicos e privados, bem como a maneira de você tecê-los juntos em um conjunto de circunstâncias ambientais é muito forte.

p.155 **Sean Griffiths** Estou interessado nessa idéia de contexto no Brasil. Quando eu olho para o contexto no Jardim Brasileiro, há uma tradição totalmente diferente da arquitetura ao seu redor- uma espécie de Português barroco. De certa forma este projeto Modernista é um esquema historicista, porque parece uma estética Le Corbusier. A torre de Le Corbusier por volta de 1930 no Rio se parece muito com este projeto. Faria algum sentido estender ou desafiar essa tradição do Modernismo no Brasil? E, se você tivesse um projeto em Bloomsbury, Londres, você estaria fazendo Classicismo Georgiano?

Robert A. M. Stern Você tem de entender que o Modernismo é uma linguagem conhecida, e você a está utilizando muito bem, mas você não pode fazer de conta que é uma idéia nova. O ponto é ter uma metodologia, não apenas um gosto.

Claire Weisz Posso interpretar diferente o seu projeto por um momento? Você está criando uma língua de construir fragmentos, ao invés de um quadro completo. Se qualquer coisa, você está interessado em pensar que a arquitetura de construir fragmentos- incluindo a estratégia na sua fachada e a qualidade da colagem dos fragmentos da paisagem- permite o avanço da linguagem do Modernismo e do clima, a fim de transformá-los em algo especial que sentimos como se fosse um lugar.

Annabelle Selldorf Este é um lugar onde as pessoas podem se mover ao oposto a uma imagem na qual existe apenas uma pessoa descansando em uma cadeira. Isto me parece ser um lugar onde as comunidades acontecem, e eu acho isso muito, muito comovente, além de todas as considerações práticas que você dá para o clima, a vista, a topografia, e assim por diante. Mais do que tudo, este projeto é um processo de demonstração.

Andy Bow Este é um projeto muito historicista e, portanto, incentiva um debate muito aberto. As imagens que você mostrou dos jardins Modernistas no Brasil são lindas, e seu manuseio do jardim na base é muito bonito. Eu poderia acreditar que é Brasileiro- pois têm jardins Brasileiros. O que eu teria desejado ver são os jardins de altura dupla no céu. Todo apartamento tem acesso a espaço exterior privado, mas as superfícies verticais são um pouquinho sem vida e poderiam ter mais interesse no indivíduo. O Brasil é um país muito extravagante. Se esse projeto fosse situado sob o céu sombrio do norte da Escócia, eu estaria aterrorizada, mas eu adoraria ver mais paisagem. Você sabia que estava abrindo um debate crítico interessante sobre Modernismo.

FASES

DISTRITO DAS ARTES BANDEIRANTES POR REBECCA GARNETT

Claire Weisz Como você cria um projeto-nessa escala para ser construído por uma única entidade- a tornar-se mais do que um loteamento?

Audrey Matlock A sua pergunta sobre as fases é interessante. Acho que houve um ou dois projetos que tiveram unidades distintas que incorporaram componentes do espaço ao ar livre, espaço comercial e espaço vivo que se alguém poderia construir e
p.157 dizer: "Aqui está uma fase que é auto-sustentável até a construção da próxima fase." Em geral, a maioria dos esquemas são bem sucedidos quando vistos completos, mas deve-se considerar também o sucesso do projeto em fases. Em muitos dos esquemas, o grande do parque central complica ainda mais a maneira pela qual o projeto poderia ter sido construído com sucesso.

Em cada proposta, deve-se pensar sobre o sucesso da primeira fase. Se você começar a construir na parte superior do local, o resultado construído seria forte o suficiente para as pessoas quererem viver lá antes de a próxima fase ser construída?

Katherine Farley Um projeto bem sucedido teria de ser feito em fases—você não poderia construir tudo de uma vez porque você estaria canibalizando seu próprio mercado, competindo com você mesmo. Em uma única fase você pode vender no bairro de 400 unidades, e então quando você tiver sessenta por cento pré-vendido, você pode começar a sua segunda fase. Baseado no sucesso da campanha de marketing, você poderia ter a construção de rolamento, o que então deixaria de ser definido por fases. Você deve pensar nas fases como pedaços de marketing. Se o mercado não está indo bem, você ainda tem que completar esse pedaço, e necessitará recursos e amenidades que irão sustentá-lo como comunidade até a próxima porção ser vendida e construída. Nos projetos que propõem parques centrais, você pode construir o parque em uma configuração provisória que pode ser adicionada com o tempo.

Audrey Matlock Você construiria o centro cultural mais cedo?

Katherine Farley Para um loteamento como este, é essencial ter um "estar lá" lá, ou então torna-se banal. Por causa do acesso limitado, o projeto deve sincronizar suas fases de construção. Como Tom

Farrell diria, comece construindo no alto—não construa os seus apartamentos na Park Avenue para depois os caminhões de concreto passarem rugindo 24 / 7. Um dos desafios dos altos arranha-céus de alta densidade é que você não pode construir cinqüenta por cento deste projeto de uma só vez. A questão de como você oferece estacionamento para estas unidades é prática e deve moldar a solução.

Patrick Bellow O paradoxo é que, em muitos projetos, se você ignora a fase de logística, você permite uma hierarquia de acesso à luz solar. Alguns dos esquemas mais bem sucedidos concluíram isso. Criando zonas tipológica com espaço estratégico, as unidades de alturas baixa, média e alta podem ter acesso à luz solar. Isso muito democrático na maneira em que a escala responde. Um paradoxo muito interessante, porque significa que no minuto em que você tentar dividir o projeto em fases, na verdade você confrontará esse paradoxo de uma maneira grandiosa.

ESCALA E PLANO DE SOLO
DISTRITO DAS ARTES BANDEIRANTES POR REBECCA GARNETT

Annabelle Selldorf Na longa seção do local há um loteamento pequenino em uma extremidade e um gigantesco na outra extremidade, o que sugere uma falta de decisão sobre o que você está realmente fazendo. O plano não tem as prioridades e as
p.158 camadas. Cidades como Berlim criam uma enorme quantidade de unidades com edifícios de dez andares que têm pátios e jardins enormes. O local é grande o suficiente para garantir esse tipo de abordagem e poderia ajudá-lo a fornecer densidade para que você tenha espaço livre para fazer um espaço urbano para a comunidade. É preciso haver uma junção do espaço e mais desejo para um espaço urbano público.

Peggy Deamer Este projeto tem uma forma consistente na qual os edifícios descem ou não para o chão—ou seja, há uma ênfase na abertura do território que tece-os todos juntos. Eles vêm para o chão com muita confiança. Eles alegam ser contextual mesmo que na verdade não sejam. Mas h á também uma escala, uma textura da fachada que vai de encontro ao solo, mesmo que o que esteja acima mude sua escala e programa.

Claire Weisz Esta estratégia não parece oferecer uma troca razoável para o que você recebe: casas de altura baixa,com terraço e que comportam uma única família. O plano precisa ser tão denso, mas está entupindo a parte inferior do local e precisa de mais jardins para as pessoas.

Andy Bow Ao reter os edifícios existentes e, em seguida, sobrepor outra geometria, muitas coisas interessantes acontecem. Todos esses pequenos pedaços têm o potencial para desdobrarem-se e serem pequenos pedaços de cidade realmente sofisticados. Mas o ponto sobre Berlim e Viena é que eles tem oito andares de altura. Pessoalmente, eu nunca gostei de ficar em pé ao lado de um grande bloco de dezesseis andares. Não me importo de ficar em de pé ao lado de torres em parques, mas quando você esta em pé ao lado de um objeto de oito andares de altura, é um objeto grande. Se você então multiplicá-lo duas ou três vezes em sua cabeça, torna-se uma escala completamente diferente. Anos atrás, eu costumava fazer grandes planos e então parti uma grande idéia. No entanto, mais e mais e mais e mais e mais em nosso escritório agora, nós falamos muito sobre os espaços que realmente gostamos e porque gostamos tanto deles.Com um pouco mais de paisagismo, eu poderia genuinamente imaginar que essa é a caminhada mais agradável de todos os esquemasque vi até agora. Mas se você também tivesse um pouco de "urban blockness" aqui, poderia informar o plano do local inteiro. O problema com a estratégia Moderna é que tantas torres são muito próximas, assim sufocando umas as outras.

Audrey Matlock Com o projeto de altura média, as proporções são certas. Muitas pessoas estão fascinadas com a idéia de levantar a borda e ter o fluxo de espaço urbano sob o edifício, e o Distrito das Artes Bandeirantes é uma maneira muito bem sucedida. Os espaços, como os passos, torna-se um espaço urbano com sombra.

Rob Rogers Estes espaços funcionam porque ambos são específicos e ambíguos—eles estão na escala de todo o complexo. Nos poucos momentos de espaço verde, posso imaginar quinze ou duas pessoas. O que é importante para o plano de solo é a densidade do tecido da paisagem e o que este pode fazer em termos de espaço numa escala de três pés de altura.

p.159
PAISAGEM
MIRANTE POR ELIZA HIGGINS

Claire Weisz A estratégia de paisagem para este projeto é a primeira que já vimos na qual a paisagem deveria preencher um propósito muito além da escala do local. É abordando algo que não é apenas sazonal, mas na verdade tem uma conexão real, potencialmente, com o rio, que agora está seco metade do tempo e não é reconhecido como um rio. Você está olhando para um pedaço de paisagem que não é apenas local. Se esse é o grande atrativo desta icônica e muito trabalhada paisagem, me pergunto por que todos os edifícios têm de ser o mesmo. Você está tratando essas edifício como infra-estrutura. Eles têm um leve toque na paisagem, e estão fornecendo o número certo de unidades e estão alimentando os espaços. Eu sinto que esse é o argumento certo, mas serão estes os edifícios certos para este argumento?

Andy Bow É universal que as pessoas amam parques, desde o Citroën Parc em Paris, ao High Line em Nova York, e ao projeto do Foreign Office, em Yokohama. As pessoas adoram quando as paisagens podem ser esculpidas para celebrar a natureza. O Mirante destaca a mudança das estações usando a paisagem para formar uma coluna central onde, em épocas diferentes do ano, transforma-se em lagoas de retenção e direciona o fluxo de água por todo o local.

Annabelle Selldorf O gesto arquitetônico neste projeto é confiante, e há uma estratégia simples no trabalho para criar espaços muito diversos. Dependendo da sua colocação dos edifícios em forma de borboleta, a relação que eles criam um ao outro fornecem uma outra dimensão.

p.160 ESCLARECIMENTOS FINAIS SOBRE INTERSECÇÕES URBANAS

p.161 **Deborah Berke** Após trabalhar neste livro e ganhar alguma perspectiva, eu percebo que o estúdio pode ter sido ainda mais produtivo do que pensei. Eu agora aprecio plenamente a força dos projetos dos alunos, a visão e capacidade de correr risco em ambos concepção e design de um projeto de empreendimento imobiliário real, complexo, e lucrativo em um local difícil e em uma cidade em constante mudança. Os projetos foram notáveis na sua atenção a detalhe e no número de aspectos de design e questões sociais abordadas. A tarefa variou em escala desde projetar unidades individuais, incluindo o layout da cozinha e acesso a ar fresco, até o planejamento de edifícios de múltiplas-unidades e a criação de uma estratégia de planejamento total. Soluções de estacionamento e acesso tiveram que ser fornecidas para milhares de carros, e a planta do local teve que enfrentar a construtibilidade de 2.500 unidades habitacionais, bem como as necessidades dos moradores. O estúdio também ponderou o design da paisagem em uma propriedade com topografia e questões de acesso difíceis. Ao final, o objetivo era criar um produto viável e comercializável que seria um sucesso no atual ambiente competitivo imobiliário da cidade de São Paulo.

Descrever qualquer projeto universitário em uma frase minimiza sua complexidade, sua profundidade, e a reflexão por trás da estratégia de design. No entanto, ao olhar como os projetos foram enfrentados e quais idéias de designs foram tomadas, alguns padrões emergiram. Muitos estudantes focaram em uma solução de altura baixa ou média, oferecendo um forte contraste com as onipresentes, anônimas torres da nova paisagem urbana de São Paulo. O projeto do distrito das artes de Becky Garnett preservou as ruínas existentes de um matadouro e reaproveitou-as como um centro criativo para uma comunidade dedicada as artes. O complexo habitacional com terraços de Anja Turowski foi também de altura baixa e denso, e criou um mundo interior abaixo das estruturas e extensa topografia verde acima.

Muito alunos assumiram o projeto dos arranha-céus de São Paulo criando torres memoráveis e mais distintas arquiteturalmente. As torres de Lis Cena cresceram de seu estilo Miesian na planta mestre moldada por preocupações ambientais. A abordagem de Catherine Anderson na construção das torres incluiu parques de arranha-céus integrais para para dar a cada residente acesso imediato a espaços verdes, criando bairros no-ar e fachadas altamente distintivas. A ousada afirmação de design de Carmel Greer utilizou uma torre de marca registrada como publicidade para a propriedade em si e propôs pistas de carros de corrida no local, em contraste com o tráfego congestionado da cidade.

A criação de espaço significativo para parque na altamente densa cidade foi outra idéia de design compartilhada entre muitos outros projetos. Hilary Zaic construiu um colar perimetrado de edifícios para preservar como terreno para parque o maior espaço central aberto possível. Eliza Higgins construiu torres em forma de bumerangue que foram carregadas-individualmente com planos de unidade inventivos; para as torres estarem dentro de um parque aquático e jardim especificamente dedicado ao gerenciamento de escape das águas durante a estação chuvosa. Os pequenos grupos de torres projetadas por Alejandro Fernandez de Mesa foram estabelecidas em uma paisagem inspirada por Burle Marx, utilizando praças interliga das para criar
p.163 diferentes escalas de espaços abertos e parques nas imediações.

Os alunos também investigaram formas de construção incomuns.Os edifícios de altura média, de densas-lajes de Bradley Baer foram torcidos e perfurados para aproveitar a ventilação e a vista na direção à sua arena de esportes sugerida. Steve Ybarra completou desenhos festivos feitos à mão que flertaram com a abordagem Venturi-Scott Brown para descrever um desenvolvimento do bairro, enquanto empurrando os limites entre arranha-céus e habitações unifamiliares separadas.

Os estudantes beneficiaram-se com a vasta experiência em empreendimento imobiliário e arquitetura de Katherine Farley, assim como (espero) os meus anos de ensino em design e sabedoria crescente que impulsionma projetos bem sucedidos em empreendimento urbano. No entanto, não há dúvida de que aprendemos tanto com cada aluno e suas variadas e corajosas abordagens quanto eles conosco.

Devemos um agradecimento enorme e apreciativo a Noé Biklen por seus ensinamentos magníficos e crítica de design focado ao longo do semestre e a Nate Shanok por sua apresentação animada e ênfase contínua sobre os perigos e prazeres do empreendimento imobiliário.

Gostaria também de agradecer a Katherine Farley e sua equipe na Tishman Speyer por sua generosidade em tempo e recursos, tanto em Nova York quanto no Brasil. Foi uma experiência significativa pois todos os alunos foram expostos a um empreendedor que valoriza a arquitetura e o processo criativo.

Finalmente, Katherine e eu gostaría-mos de agradecer a Edward Bass por seu conhecimento grandioso na criação de Edward P. Bass Distinguished Visiting architecture Fellowship, que tornou possível este estúdio.

-Deborah Berke, Professora, Escola de Arquitetura Yale

p.164 BIOGRAFIAS

p.165 **Patrick Bellew** é o principal fundador do Atelier Ten, engenheiros ambientais, com base em Londres e Nova York. Em 2010, ele foi o EeroSaarinen Visiting Professor na Yale School of Architecture, onde foi professor visitante desde 2001. Ele lecionou na Architectural Association, na Bartlett School of Architecture, na University of Reading, e na De Montfort University, em Leicester. Seu trabalho no Atelier Ten ganhou reconhecimento internacional por sua expertise em estratégias sustentáveis e sistemas de integração ambiental. Bellew é um administrador do Green Building Council do Reino Unido e recebeu o prêmio Designer Real para Indústria em 2010, bem como a medalha Happold Medal em 2008. Em 2004, ele foi eleito membro da Royal Academy of Engineering em Londres.

Andy Bow é sócio sênior da Foster + Partners. Desde que ingressou neste escritório em 1996, ele gerenciou equipes de design para inúmeros projetos de alto perfil, tanto em Londres quanto no exterior. Ele foi professor e lecionou em mais de trinta escolas de arquitetura e tem sido um RIBA examinador externo na Bartlett School of Architecture nos últimos oito anos. Em 2010, ele foi o Eero Saarinen Professor visitante na Yale School of Architecture. Em 2000, foi juiz do RIBA Bronze e Silver que oferecia medalhas para estudantes. Bow estudou arquitetura na Mackintosh School of Architecture em Glasgow.

Peggy Deamer é diretora na empresa Deamer Stúdio. Ela é um professora na Yale School of Architecture, onde leciona desenho e história/teoria. Ela lecionou na Cooper Union, da University of Kentucky, Barnard College, da Columbia University, e da University of Princeton. Seus artigos têm aparecido em *Assemblage, Praxis, Perspecta and Drawings/Buildins/Text*. Seu seminário e estúdio na Yale foram publicados no livro *Millennium House* (The Monacelli Press, 2004.)Ela foi a co-editora da *Re-Reading Perspecta* and *Building (in) the Future: Recasting Labor in Architecture* (MIT Press 2010). Ela recebeu seu mestrado em arquitetura e doutorado da Princeton University.

Sean Griffiths é diretor e co-fundador do Fashion Architecture Taste (FAT), uma clínica de arte e arquitetura baseada em Londres, Inglaterra. Griffiths tem ensinado e lecionado em instituições em todo o mundo, incluindo a University of Westminster e na Yale School of Architecture. Ele escreveu artigos para CABE e RIBA e contribuiu para livros, jornais,e revistas internacionalmente. Griffiths estudou arquitetura em Manchester Polytechnic and the Polytechnic na área Central de Londres. Em 2008, ele e seus parceiros na FAT lecionaram no Estúdio Bass e am 2010 retornaram como professores visitantes.

Vanessa Grossman é arquiteta, e também é graduada na Escola de Arquitetura e Urbanismo da Universidade de São Paulo. Ela tem mestrado em história da arquitetura da Paris 1 Pantheon-Sorbonne University. Ela é atualmente candidata a Ph.D. em história, teoria e crítica em arquitetura na Princeton University, onde está fazendo uma pesquisa sobre interseções entre política, arquitetura e urbanismo em ambos França e Brasil pós-guerra.

Ela é a autora do livro *A arquitetura e o urbanismo revisitados pela Internacional Situacionista* (São Paulo: p.166 Annablume; FAPESP, 2006). Seu trabalho apareceu na *L'architecture d'Aujourd'hui, AMC, Archistorm, Area, and Pidgin*.

Tom Farrell é diretor administrativo sênior da Tishman Speyer e, nos últimos 16 anos, teve um papel de liderança no desenvolvimento de projetos de arranha-céus, incluindo a Torre Norte, em São Paulo, a Torre Hearst, em Nova Iorque, e a revitalização de espaços públicos e comerciais no Rockefeller Center. É membro da diretoria do Congresso dos Construtores de Nova Iorque York e do ACE Program da Grande Nova Iorque. Farrell é um engenheiro profissional licenciado e tem um grau de bacharel em engenharia civil pela Manhattan College, onde ele faz parte do conselho de curadores.

Audrey Matlock é fundadora da Audrey Matlock Architect, com sede em Nova Iorque e Sag Harbor, NY. Seu escritório é especializado em projetos residenciais, culturais e empresariais tanto localmente quanto no exterior. Sua empresa tem sido reconhecida por excelência em design pelo American Institute of Architects, a Architectural League of New York, a International Interior Design Association, e a Society of American Registered Architects. Antes de estabelecer sua própria firma em 1993, Matlock trabalhou na Skidmore Owings & Merrill, bem como na Perkins + Will, onde foi diretora de design. Ela tem um mestrado da Yale School of Architecture.

Cathleen McGuigan é crítica de arquitetura, jornalista cultural, e professora. Além de ser uma colaboradora de longa data a revista Newsweek, seus artigos têm aparecido em revistas como *The New York Times Magazine, Smithsonian, Rolling Stone*, e *Harpers Bazaar*. Na primavera de 2011, foi nomeada editora-chefe da *Architectural Record* Magazine. Ela é professora adjunta na Graduate School of Journalism na Columbia University e foi Loeb Fellow na Harvard University School of Design. McGuigan é bacharel em arte pela Brown University. Ela era uma Poynter Fellow em Yale na primavera de 2011.

Rob Rogers começou sua parceria em arquitetura com Jonathan Marvel em 1992. Antes do RMA, Rogers trabalhou no I.M. Pei & Partners, onde contribuiu para projetos incluindo o Grande Louvre, em Paris, e do Banco da China, em Hong Kong. Rogers lecionou em estúdios de design no Pratt Institute, Columbia University, Harvard University, Parsons School of Design, e Washington University. Ele é membro nobre para o U.S. General Services Administration's Design Excellence Program e serve numerosas organizações profissionais locais e estaduais. Rogers é bacharel em artes e tem uma licenciatura em arquitetura pela Rice University, e recebeu seu mestrado com distinção em design da Harvard Graduate School of Design.

Annabelle Selldorf é diretora da Selldorf Architects, baseada em Nova Iorque. Sua firma, fundada em 1988, é especializada em projetos culturais e relacionados a arte, incluindo o Neue Gallerie New York: Museum for German and Austrian Art, a Gladstone Gallery, também em Nova Iorque, e a renovação do Sterling e Francine Clark Art Institute, na Williams College, p.167 Massachusetts. Ela é bacharel em arquitetura pela Pratt Institute e seu mestrado é em arquitetura pela Syracuse University. Ela é membro do American Institute of Architects e presidente do conselho de administração da Architectural League de Nova Iorque.

Nate Shanok é o diretor de aquisições da Tishman Speyer em São Paulo, onde dirige novos investimentos no Brasil, administra disposições para os portfólio atuais de escritórios comerciais de investimentos, e coordena atividades de levantamento de capital. Shanok ingressou na empresa em 2005 como parte do programa de desenvolvimento de liderança, durante a qual ele ajudou a subscrever várias aquisições em Boston, Chicago e Washington, DC, e auxiliou na formação da Tishman Speyer China Fund. Graduado pela Syracuse University, ele é um membro antigo de consultoria de seu programa internacional de estudos no exterior, e serviu o conselho da High School for Leadership and Public Service, em Nova Iorque. Ele recebeu um MBA pela Kellogg School of Management da Northwestern University.

Claire Weisz é sócia-fundadora da WXY arquitetura + urbanismo. Weisz está no corpo docente da NYU Wagner School of Public Policy e lecionou na Yale University, Columbia University, e Pratt Institute's School of Architecture . Em 2004, ela foi co-editora da edição AD "Extreme Sites:Greening the Brownfield." Weisz recebeu seu diploma de graduação da University of Toronto e seu mestrado em arquitetura pela Yale.